A Hundred Years
of
Fishy Skulduggery

How the Crown acquired the fishing rights of three Selkirk Estates, Philiphaugh, the Haining, and the Selkirk Burgh Common Good, charged for them and had to give them back because they didn't own them.

A Fishing Story

The Ettrick Water as it runs through Selkirk

(photo courtesy of Janis Cornwall)

This is the remarkable story of how a small group of fishing enthusiasts, the Angling Association from Selkirk, won back salmon fishing rights on the Ettrick Water - a river in the Borders of Scotland and tributary of the Tweed - which the Burgh had had for hundreds of years. The rights had been taken over in doubtful circumstances in 1912 by the Crown's representatives and were regained in 2016. The tale spans two centuries and ended after 24 years of dogged research, single-minded campaigning and a great deal of luck. It involved three estates and a total of roughly five miles of leased fishing rights on both banks of the river. It is essentially the story of a long legal battle.

What the Crown charged £1 for in 1912 became £4,700 in 2003. We didn't think that was right!

This is how it happened.

Beware of barking at underdogs; don't fight

with people who have nothing to lose.

DORY PREVIN

A HUNDRED YEARS OF FISHY SKULDUGGERY

First published in 2021
Copyright © Dr Lindsay D Neil, June 2021

ISBN No. 978-1-8382270-1-2

Contents

(continued overleaf)

NOTE: *I apologise in advance if the reader may feel a sense of repetition as the story unfolds.*
"This is the lesson: never give in, never give in, never, never, never, never…"
– Winston Churchill

Preface

After a decision was taken in 1992 to investigate and perhaps challenge the Crown's claim of ownership of the fishing rights in the Ettrick dating back to 1910, we were clueless as to the scale of the task ahead. We did not realise that from the outset it would require such a lot of painstaking research, such a mountain of correspondence and seemingly endless persuasion. Not only that but that it would take such a long time. The Crown Estates Commission finally recognised in early 2016 that all of the salmon fishing rights on the River Ettrick where it runs through Selkirk did not actually belong to them. They had undertaken their own enquiries about these rights in 1910, never completed them, but despite this had formally and incorrectly claimed ownership of them in 1912. At that time the Crown Estates were called 'HM Woods, Forests and Land Revenues' (HMW), before becoming the Crown Estates Commission (CEC) in 1924.

Furthermore, it was emphatically demonstrated (but never plainly admitted) that the Crown Estates (CEC) had absolutely no legal basis in Scots law on which to be charging Selkirk anglers, up to very recently, for a lease to fish in the Ettrick for the fishing rights that the Crown wrongly claimed to own. That claim ended in 2016.

The CEC had, in more recent times, brazenly been doing this following their original claim when their predecessors issued the lease to Selkirk Burgh Council (SBC) in 1912. They had done so while at the same time originally giving written assurances that the fishing rights would be investigated to establish their true ownership.

Immediately before 1912 it had cost Selkirk residents nothing to fish in the Ettrick, only their small annual subscription to the local angling club. They were not best pleased when the Crown heavy-handedly claimed to own them and charged them money for what they had enjoyed virtually without cost for as long as anyone could remember.

During our research, we uncovered three miraculous things: the undiscovered Philiphaugh Charter, the Glasgow document hoard, and the wonderful salmon poacher of Selkirk, all significant in moving our investigation forward. However, as the fact-finding got underway in 1992 we were unaware that we were about to encounter the 'Establishment' using all their powers to deflect an inconvenient 'disturbance' in their affairs.

Us - The Selkirk and District Angling Association.

Prologue

Before embarking on this prolonged and tortuous journey, it may be helpful to paint a quick literary picture of the background to the cuts, thrusts and parries that comprised the battles to recover what was ours.

First, a brief word on salmon fishing in Scotland. River fish, i.e. salmon – or as they are described in legal documents 'salmon or migratory fish of the salmon kind' – have long been part of the Scottish national diet and that of many other peoples since before the dawn of history. River fishing historically had also had considerable importance in Roman times. It was the Romans who gave the name 'Salmo'* to the biggest and the once very common river fish from which we in turn derived the name that we still use, the 'salmon'.

Salmon and their near-relatives, sea trout, were revered in Norse mythology. The Vikings believed that by eating them they conferred wisdom upon themselves. Later on, in mediaeval times, salmon progressed from being simply a local food source to becoming commercially significant, especially in Scotland. Wild river salmon were to become a marketable product for sale locally to the people of larger towns in Scotland, to England and for export overseas.

The overseas trade and that to England involved the fish being preserved. After preservative salting they were packed into wooden barrels (a filled barrel weighed 14 stones = 89 Kilos or 196 lbs) and, after satisfying the local demand, were then even exported to the nearby European continent from the River Tweed communities. The salmon had became an important trading commodity, much in demand as a food source in the Scottish Borders and was a harvest available in great abundance and easily caught.

As an example of this plentiful supply, it was considered necessary to include in some local agricultural contracts, where a farmer undertook to provide the food for his employee, a limit of only two days per week when a hiring farmer could feed his tenant workers or 'bondagers' on salmon. Such contract provisions were not unusual in the 19th century.

Prior to the industrial revolution and before the burgeoning of Victorian industry and population led to widespread river pollution, salmon in plenty continued to be the happy situation on all sizeable watercourses in the UK. There were seemingly limitless numbers of salmon in Britain and throughout Europe. However, the right to fish for salmon since ancient times was one of the privileges that a monarch could bestow on those he favoured. Fishermen could not simply throw a line into the water and catch salmon indiscriminately. These rights were usually jealously guarded by those who owned them. Many court battles were fought down the ages to determine ownership.

Selkirk had hung on to its rights since the first mention of fishing in the Ettrick in the 12th Century at the time of the foundation of Scotland's first abbey. Now it was being challenged.

Selkirk and District Angling Association (SAA)

Formed in approximately 1860, the fishermen were originally simply the Selkirk Angling Association. Later on, the title was extended to include the 'District' which it is today.

Membership was restricted to 60 persons only and the cost minimal.

Annual medal presented to the most outstanding fishermen of Selkirk Angling Association. First presented in 1860

Various annual competitions were organised both within Selkirk and against surrounding towns. Bat Tyson (see later) won the above medal in 1888. Bat Tyson was a colourful 19th century poacher whose actions from the grave gave us the ammunition we needed to defeat the Crown. He proved more useful to Selkirk than either St. Zeno or St Andrew, the traditional patron saints of fishermen and anglers!

---

* Salmo – salmonis; m. Pliny = Salmon - Cassell's Latin Dictionary.

Map of the Burgh of Selkirk, showing estates as they border the river and shows the extent of Fishing Rights in 1914. See also map on p 20. The river is in blue. The length of the lease was 2½ miles but the rights on each bank were separately owned adding up to 5 miles in total.

4

Introduction

Salmon fishing by the late 20th century had by and large become the exclusive province of the rich or those who could afford the hefty charges imposed by proprietors who owned the right to fish on their stretch of a river. Even today it remains an elite sport enjoyed by the few who either owned their own stretch or could afford to pay many hundreds of pounds sterling to the owner for the permission to fish for a day or more for salmon on his 'beat' or portion of the river.

By the late nineteenth century catching and eating salmon was no longer regarded locally as a readily free and available source of food *(Ref 18)*. By the late twentieth century and since the advent of widespread salmon farming, 'cheap' salmon was once again accessible to all and continues to be so. In the interim, proprietors made a substantial income from selling short term licences to anyone wanting to fish their river. However, over-exploitation of river fish had become increasingly damaging to fish stocks during the latter 20th and early 21st centuries. Abundance of a food supply which had been the norm for most of the 20th century was now less important as nearly all fish when caught are returned to the rivers in order to try to maintain the existing local fish populations, such is the modern scarcity of wild river fish. In an effort to enhance fish numbers, the seasonal netting of Tweed salmon returning to spawn has been radically reduced in recent years.

Salmon numbers are increasing in only a few individual rivers throughout the UK and on the whole they are diminishing rapidly. An attempt to halt the decline, besides returning fish caught, also included the enforced reduction of pollution by limiting industrial waste, sewage releases and the run off from chemically treated arable land. Despite these measures the overall trend is still downwards: fewer salmon are available for the angling fraternity to catch.

A new factor impacting upon returning spawning Atlantic salmon is the largely uncontrolled harvesting of salmon by trawlers off Greenland and the Faroe Islands. These fish, recent research has established, are the ones most of which would eventually return to Scottish rivers to breed.

This discovery was made by radio-tagging and tracing the migratory fish. It is where Scottish salmon go after leaving their 'birth' rivers, and after three years on average most of them come back to their 'birth' rivers to spawn.

A further negative factor is the alleged effect of a plague of sea-lice due to the parasite multiplying where there is salt water salmon farming. The sea lice epidemic may be responsible for up to 30% wastage of the salmon crop in Scottish fish farms. The use of emamectin, neonicotinoids and other chemicals to control sea lice are now known to inflict widespread damage to marine ecology and may also contribute to the overall fall in salmon numbers. A more ecological solution is the introduction of a variety of wrasse, a type of fish bred for the purpose because they feed on sea lice.

Gyrodactylus Salaris, the salmon fluke, has ravaged salmon populations in Northern European rivers in the last 50 years. It cannot survive in salt water in sea water concentrations and as yet it has not known to have migrated to the UK. Because of the lack of success of treatment methods, it may only be a matter of time before it is accidentally imported via rainbow trout on which it can survive.

Salmon were plentiful in most Scottish rivers in the 19th century and there were enough fish for all. The local people in Selkirk were able to help themselves to a bountiful food source in the Ettrick Water and were largely left unmolested in this pursuit until the beginning of the twentieth century.

The authorities in London with their prevalent hunger for ownership and regulation decided to disrupt the fishing harmony that existed for the fishermen of the Royal Burgh of Selkirk. They wanted ownership and control of the salmon fishing around Selkirk. This desire may have been an inherited trait from those who had successfully colonised and already dominated much of the world. With their legacy of Victorian acquisitiveness and their largely patrician background, ultimately they largely succeeded.

The year they started was 1910.

This account concerns the right to fish in the River Ettrick, known locally as 'Ettrick Water' or just 'the Ettrick'. With the Yarrow, which joins it a little above Selkirk, the Ettrick is a major tributary of the Tweed, and together they join it near to Galashiels. The two rivers, the Yarrow and the Ettrick, are now collectively known as the Ettrick and run through the middle of Selkirk before joining the Tweed. That is how the original ancient fishing rights belonging to Selkirk arose. The rights to fish the river running through Selkirk belonged to the actual people of Selkirk from time immemorial.

The representatives of the Crown in 1910 sought to own those rights which had been handed down to Selkirk people "unsullied and untarnished" for hundreds of years, and set about acquiring them by any means whatsoever.

This is the true story of the contest in which a number of local citizens from the small, ancient town of Selkirk in the Scottish Borders – with a rich and sometimes bloody history stretching back well over 1000 years – took on powerful adversaries who were denying them their traditional rights and imposed controls on what they and their forefathers had enjoyed for centuries.

The Selkirk folk wanted to hang on to their free fishing and preserve it for the future. They refused to accept the sustained autarchy and domination by a large, authoritatively influential and august national institution trying to deny them their rights. The institution which questioned the Selkirk citizen's rights in 1910 was then called 'HM Woods, Forests and Land Revenues,' (HMW). It subsequently became the Crown Estates Commission in 1924. HMW wrote a letter both to Philiphaugh Estate and to Selkirk Burgh Council and started it off *(see Appendix A)*.

HMW from the outset appeared to be determined to control and dominate as much as they could, not only Selkirk Burgh's rights but neighbouring ones as well. HMW represented the Crown and ran various other properties in Scotland, comprising both fishing rights and pieces of real estate. All of these were claimed by the British Crown as its property by right. The driving forces behind HMW were landowners and others from the upper, titled classes. It became a contest between a few 'Davids' and many 'Goliaths'.

As in the biblical story, David soundly thrashed Goliath. But whereas in the bible story David smote Goliath only once, which was enough, this modern Goliath needed to be smitten many times over during an extended period before he would submit, desert the battlefield and retire to nurse his wounds.

In the various avenues and many cul-de-sacs along which it was necessary for us to travel in order to complete an unassailable case to achieve our aim, there will be areas that other communities may find helpful. Our researches may provide ammunition in their own battles against a seemingly respectable and overwhelming power with almost unlimited resources of expertise and finance behind them.

The Selkirk fishermen were very determined and steadfast in their belief of their ancient right to fish the river Ettrick, but for many years they had done little to assert their rights. There was no need to do so, it wasn't in question nor costing much. They were all members of the Selkirk and District Angling Association (hereinafter SAA). The simple qualification for membership of the SAA was to live within the Selkirk Burgh boundaries, although the number of members was limited to 60 persons in toto and was only open to those who paid their annual subs but it was enough. The annual subscriptions were minimal at the outset, still only eight shillings and sixpence (42½p) in 1939.

Over time, these doughty men of Selkirk became more and more resentful of the increasing and ultimately exorbitant leasing charges imposed by the CEC who succeeded HMW. They questioned the Crown's right to demand them and after much thought, in view of the potential cost of litigation, eventually chose to contest them.

What had been regarded as an affordable and acceptable financial burden on the SAA throughout most of the 20th century, increased and became heavier and more unaffordable by the onset of the 21st. This escalation of the leasing charges may have been partly due to a new revenue-enhancing policy adopted by the CEC seeking to maximise their income. What had cost £1 in 1912 became £4,700 by 2003.

It is worth noting that in contrast to more recent times, income had not originally been the principal reason for CEC's predecessors claiming ownership in 1912 – then it was simply a wish to extend their power, influence and control. The initial leasing charges proposed were pretty small.

The individual executives who administered HMW were already wealthy people, and the Crown possessions were already extensive and remunerative. At this early stage they were simply aiming to gain control where they believed they could do so unopposed.

Ultimately, many years later, it did become an issue of money – money that some members of the SAA couldn't afford. The members of the SAA remained convinced that they were in the right regarding the free access to fish and that the autocrats and aristocrats in faraway London who imposed the increased charges, were in the wrong. So they decided to set out to prove it.

The Hundred Years War between England and France had lasted for 116 years, from 1337 until 1453. It had many phases and was basically about English nobility trying to retain ownership of land and titles in France. The French kings objected and largely succeeded in expelling the English.

The campaign to re-establish the traditional salmon fishing rights of Selkirk folk lasted almost as long – 106 years from its outset in 1910 until 2016, and was also about ownership of property and likewise had several phases. Akin to the war with France, the modern hundred years' war between Selkirk anglers and the CEC also straddled two centuries from its birth in 1910 through to its conclusion in 2016. It was Selkirk's own mini Hundred

Years War. Selkirk won, but the CEC, although they had comprehensively lost, had still not acknowledged defeat by 2018. The CEC's loss certainly cost them a great deal in legal fees, that much they admitted but it turned out to have been money they had wasted in trying to defend the indefensible.

Anyone who enjoys following the ins and outs of legal proceedings and the twists and turns of the evidence as the case unfolds will hopefully find this book diverting.

There were three astonishing coincidences that might suggest that divine approval for our campaign had been accorded to us! This of course was not the case but the finds we made – each at a crucial point in the campaign – were, for us, extraordinary strokes of good fortune. There will be more on that later in the narrative. The readers can judge for themselves whether they were supernatural or not!

Although essentially a seemingly very dry subject with many cul-de-sacs this legal adventure is highly instructive. For the inquisitors it was utterly fascinating. Happily, at no point on our long journey were we required to enter a courtroom or sustain the horrendous financial burden of legal fees by formally going to law. By salting money away the SAA had prepared for that risk but in the end this turned out to be a grass roots mission carried out successfully at very little cost to the SAA.

It was however undertaken with the best possible legal advice. A Queen's Counsel with a keen interest in fishing and with a wide and varied career behind him, crucially navigated a path for us through the heavily mined legal territory. I refer, of course, to Sheriff Kevin Drummond, the Sheriff of Selkirkshire.*

Kevin and I were already fishing companions: we were members of a syndicate which

---

*[The Sheriffdom of Selkirkshire is an ancient post, first recorded in 1265 when a local 'laird' called 'Andrew de Synton' was appointed to it by King Richard the Lion. Synton is an extinct barony situated about four miles south of Selkirk. There has been a sheriff continuously carrying out the role since then, a length of time of approximately 750 years. Sheriff Drummond is now, in 2018, retired.]

shared a boat on one of the lochs on a local estate. As a friend, a former tenant on the Tweed at Bemersyde and as a member of SAA he made it clear from the outset that he could not be involved in the case in his capacity as Sheriff. He would, however, be able to assist us in our researches in a private capacity in matters of law.

For us to be able to draw on Kevin's wide experience and high qualifications was a bit like having access to the Ultra secret secured by the code-cracking team at Bletchley Park in WWII. We were able to match and resist any legal arm-twisting within the comfort of knowing we were authoritatively and legally right. We had unfettered access to legal 'jewellery'.

The whole saga represents the best of spontaneous local community motivation and cooperation which generally only materialises when there is something worth fighting for. That is what it was for Selkirk.

While researching we discovered that a well-known habitual Selkirk poacher and fisherman had, by his actions in 1892, caused the law of the country to be changed, inadvertently proved our case for us, and ultimately caused the last part of the Crown's case to collapse.

Salmon in the Scottish Borders: the monetary aspect

The Tweed river system was the principal source of salmon in the Borders but, in contrast to the section of the main river downstream from Kelso, the inland stretches of Borders rivers were not a great source of salmon in terms of a marketable food commodity. Most commercial exploitation took place at the mouths of rivers, in our case the Tweed, mainly by netting and trapping, not rod and line fishing by individuals as elsewhere. Ease of access to rail and sea transportation was an important factor in determining where salmon could be marketed, as was local demand *(ref 18)*.

The beneficiaries, of what markets there were, were the landowners and owners of netting rights. There was a thriving local industry dependant on taking salmon from the Tweed from the downstream beats but little of commercial significance upstream from Kelso. Most of it took place round the mouth of the Tweed.

It was noted in 1805 that 15,000 salmon had been sent from Berwick to London in one single week which illustrates the sheer scale of the contemporary trade! These fish were gathered by harvesting the migrating ones, and coastal towns - Berwick in particular - had good transport and communications and thus dominated the local Borders and wider markets.

Even though the main hauls of salmon were being landed downstream from Kelso and, besides being a ready source of food, salmon rights were nevertheless also highly valued in the upper Tweed and its tributaries, particularly so in the 19th and 20th centuries.

Fishing upstream was mainly by rod and line. Money was made by landowners leasing out the liberty to fish on their waters for sport. Most of the salmon fishing rights were possessed by local landowners having been originally acquired from the monarch by old charters or sometimes by private purchase on the open market. Some ancient burghs, and Selkirk amongst them, owned fishing rights on nearby rivers through the possession of a Common Good, i.e. the property of the indigenous inhabitants of the Burgh. This will be explained later.

As a food source, even if episodic, it was realised from ancient times that the value lay in the salmon's abundance, seasonal dependability and also latterly to its exclusivity. In the nineteenth and twentieth centuries only those individuals who paid money to the owners of rights were permitted to fish, and that excluded many Borders folk from an important food source. In this respect, Selkirk was very lucky to have its own river in which to fish.

Salmon fishing had the potential for wealth generation for whoever owned the rights to fish for the salmon in the Tweed and also the many lesser rivers where salmon came to spawn. It also encouraged poaching as there was a ready market for illegally caught salmon. For that reason these rights were fiercely guarded by their fortunate owners. Battles were joined over salmon fishing rights and many court actions fought over them. Most profitable was the netting industry carried out at the mouth of the Tweed, but in the latter part of the 20th century this had been deliberately reduced to almost nothing by the need to try to sustain the dwindling fish population and buying out the netting rights. Sadly, the reduction in netting appears to have made little difference to the decline.

Because poaching had been very common, laws were introduced between 1771 and 1807 in an attempt to limit, apprehend and punish poachers. The laws by modern standards were draconian, manifestly unfair and unscrupulously applied but more of that later on in this account. The happy state of affairs for the Selkirk folk was that they could fish the lower river Ettrick for free because it was part of their ancient common heritage, secured in part by a grant charter of 1535/6.* As a result this confirmed that they themselves as Selkirk residents owned the fishing rights on the river running through Selkirk.

---

 * The charter from King James V to Selkirk was granted on 4th March, 1535. Actually, before 1752, the new year started on March 25th. The year of the charter was therefore 1536. (Julian to Gregorian calendar) (Ref 13)

Phase I

How it started

In 1910, HM Woods, Forests and Land Revenues, (subsequently the Crown Estates Commission, CEC), an enormous and extremely rich UK national organisation representing and administering the lands and property of the British Crown, fired the first shots. Based in sumptuous premises in London, they were keen to establish their ownership of Selkirk Burgh's and all the nearby fishing rights which they claimed was necessary in order to rationalise rights to fish for salmon on several stretches of the river Ettrick.

No attempt was made to regulate the parts of the Ettrick belonging to the Duke of Buccleuch above Selkirk nor the part just below Selkirk belonging to Sunderland Hall Estate and the Scott-Plummer family. Both were owned by noble families.

When they first suggested that they might claim them, their stated aim was so that they would then be able to amalgamate the rights into a simplified single lease to Selkirk Burgh, discourage poaching and what they termed "pollution". Admittedly, their main motivation at that time was for administrative dominance and not for money, but later in the 20th century, that would change.

The rights they claimed comprised salmon fishing pertaining to the three stretches of the River Ettrick which was where the Selkirk anglers fished. The rights were owned respectively by the Philiphaugh Estate, the Haining Estate and lastly the stretch owned by the people of Selkirk embodied in the Selkirk Common Good Fund. ('Common Good' is an ancient inheritance from mediaeval times of property owned by the residents of a burgh and administered by the Burgh Council. Many burghs in Scotland have 'Common Goods'.) After much correspondence and argument, a comprehensive lease of all three fishing rights to Selkirk Burgh Council was eventually signed by the council in 1914 *(see Appendices A – original enquiry, and C, The Burgh Council reluctantly signs).*

What prompted HMW to claim what was not theirs?

It is difficult for us in the 21st Century to understand the motives and attitudes of the men who were determined to exert their control over what had been well managed and happy fishing arrangements between landlords, fishermen, the law and the local Burgh authorities up until 1910. It was working perfectly well under the stewardship of the local anglers who had Selkirk Burgh Council's approval to do so; the owners were happy and the law (although rather ineffectively) regularly intervened to discourage poaching which was at a tolerable level.

Just before the First World War, the British ruled the oceans, dominated a quarter of the World's population and much of its land. The British Empire was at its height. The class system prospered, land ownership, privilege and titles, besides military power, were the unchallenged instruments that permitted domination of peoples and affairs both in this country and abroad in the Empire. The arrangements appeared to work well and were generally tolerated. Few questions were asked of those who were in charge of the UK government and the respect for one's 'betters' was deeply instilled into the national psyche and the behaviour patterns of the average citizen.

It is therefore perhaps understandable that amongst those 'superior beings' involved in administering affairs of state that a mindset existed that was a manifestation of what are now the less acceptable facets of class distinction and privilege. It was then prevalent and accepted as an unquestioned superiority of rank and authority. So it would have been unremarkable among the ruling classes to look for and find areas over which they could widen and extend their administrative influence. They would have believed that they had a right to do so.

It should be remembered that the accepted mindset of the age allowed a disproportionate and mindless slaughter of Scots in WWI. Selkirk itself lost almost 300 of its young men – roughly 17% of those of working age – out of a total population of 7400. One quarter of all

Scots serving in the Forces in WWI were killed. There was a lot to think about besides ancient rights to fish, and authority was respected. Individuals and government commanded and the population obediently followed.

Between the unquestioned fishing rights owned by the Duke of Buccleuch and those of the downstream estate, Sunderland Hall, owned by the Scott-Plummers, there was a stretch of the Ettrick, the fishing rights of which were owned by the Burgh of Selkirk and two small estates. It was this stretch that was to be the target of HMW.

With little regard for the rights and wrongs of the ownership, HMW relentlessly engineered the dispossession of these rights both by claiming the ownership and by failing to undertake any investigations which would have shown them to be in the wrong. HMW acted presumably in the knowledge that their assertions would not be resolutely opposed by a small Borders burgh and some small landowners, one of whom showed little interest in their possession of fishing rights. Eventually they succeeded in their quest to possess and control, but, in the end, we proved them to be in serious error.

How we approached the problem

The Selkirk and District Angling Association (SAA), as previously mentioned, had been in existence since at least 1860 and membership required a small subscription. (In 1937, it was only 5 shillings per annum.) The members fished the Ettrick and Yarrow for trout and the Ettrick alone for salmon. Part of their role was to monitor, control and husband the salmon fishing in the Ettrick.

The SAA fished both banks of about 2½ miles of the Ettrick for salmon, but we were primarily interested in that part of the stretch where the Ettrick runs through Selkirk and we believed belonged to the town. Our early research was directed to this important part of the whole lease that was relevant to us and was what was known locally as 'The Town Water'. Initially we were not aware of the Philiphaugh Estate's interest *(see map p.20)*.

16

From being initially unaware that more than Selkirk's fishing rights were being challenged, we soon discovered that the adjoining part of the river upstream from Selkirk was also involved. This was the privately-owned Philiphaugh Estate Water which had been part of the overall stretch of river traditionally fished by Selkirk fishermen. We found out that Philiphaugh had also had their fishing rights challenged and that their ownership was being questioned at the same time and in much the same way as Selkirk's *(see maps p.23)*.

Now that we knew that the parts of the river usually fished by Selkirk anglers included the Estate's property besides the Burgh's, it was sensible to consider and examine the rights claimed by HMW on the river as a whole.

It was of course essential to obtain the Estate's approval to investigate a case and aim collectively to submit our results to the CEC. That was quickly and easily secured. Sir Michael Strang Steel, owner of Philiphaugh, was happy for the angling club's researchers to enquire into the Philiphaugh rights alongside their own. So the campaign set off initially to claim back both the rights on the Selkirk Burgh and Philiphaugh stretches of river together.

It was only much later in the saga that we found it necessary to investigate the Haining Estate's rights because we had understood initially, and were authoritatively told several times, that the Crown owned the Haining Estate's fishings outright.

Crucial to the success of the campaign was the fortuitous occurrence of the three amazing discoveries, mentioned earlier (Preface), which were akin to the discovery of multiple crocks of gold! We were spurred on and much encouraged as we recognised the relevance to our case of each crock as it was unearthed.

To set the scene

It had always been the strongly held belief amongst Selkirk folk that simply by living in the Burgh they possessed the right to fish the River Ettrick for salmon. It had never been questioned before and the 1536 charter confirmed it.

This belief was reinforced by the undisputed fact that part of the river they habitually fished actually ran through Selkirk Common Good land. The land had been owned (beneficially) by the townspeople for centuries and was enshrined in a still extant King James IV act of 1491 and the subsequent 1535/6 Burgh Charter of King James V confirmed that it was part of the Burgh's 'Common Good' *(see p4 map – Common Land is outlined red. Ref 13).*

Common Good Act 1491
1491 c.19 Act of King James IV

Of the common gud of all burrowis.

C2 This Act is listed in 12mo edition as 1491 c.36

Item it is statut and ordinit that the commoune gud of all our souerane lordis burrowis within the realme be obseruit and kepit to the commoune gude of the toune and to be spendit in commoune And necessare thingis of the burght be the avise of the consale of the toune for the tyrne and dekkynnis of ctaftis quhare thai ar ... Fl

---

The original Act governing Common Good property, still operative in 2020

The townsfolk, when asked about it, were an ample source of oral evidence. They and their forebears had fished in the Ettrick and that during the 19th century the control and administration of these fisheries had been traditionally entrusted to Selkirk Burgh Council. The Council, in their turn, had passed on the running of the fishing to the Selkirk and District Angling Association, the SAA.

The Selkirk people could not believe that HMW (the subsequently named Crown Estates Commission, CEC) had any business interfering with their ancient rights and greatly resented their actions. From the evidence gleaned from old Burgh council records, the townsfolk and its council were 'fair black affronted' when HMW first challenged their ownership, but this was an age when one hesitated to question authority and class was the determinant social denominator *(see Appendix C).*

A letter was sent to the Selkirk Burgh Council, according to council minutes, and was similar to the first part of the one which had been sent to Philiphaugh Estate. HMW were seeking information on how the Burgh Council owned the fishing rights in Selkirk but unlike the letter to Philiphaugh it did not suggest that some form of affidavit or evidence from the Council of public access to fishing would confirm their title. *(Appendix A)*

Copy of the original correspondence sent to the lawyers representing Philiphaugh Estate (part of the 'Glasgow Hoard'), a more peremptory letter was received by Selkirk Burgh Council requesting information. It was only in 2005 that we discovered that the Crown Authorities in 1910 had known all along that Philiphaugh was a barony with ownership of fishings'

PRO 23
A

Copy

Office of H. M. Woods &c.
1 Whitehall S. W.
18th November 1910

File S. 3627

Gentlemen,

Salmon Fishings, River Ettrick, Philiphaugh

With reference to your letter of the 10th instant I am directed by Sir Stafford Howard to state that in the absence of any other available documentary evidence, a statutory declaration by Mr Steel himself if he has been in possession of the Estate for 20 years will be accepted to the effect that he holds the lands by Barony title and actually exercised the right of Salmon Fishing to the exclusion of all other persons for at least 20 years, within limits to be clearly defined on the Ordnance Maps herewith, which should be referred to in the declaration.

The method of fishing should also be mentioned.

If the Maps do not show the whole of the lands further sheets will be sent to you on your specifying the numbers of the sheets required.

It should of course be made clear in the declaration to which bank the claim attaches.

I am
Gentlemen
Your obedient Servant

Messrs A. J. & A. Graham   (Sgd) Morton Evans

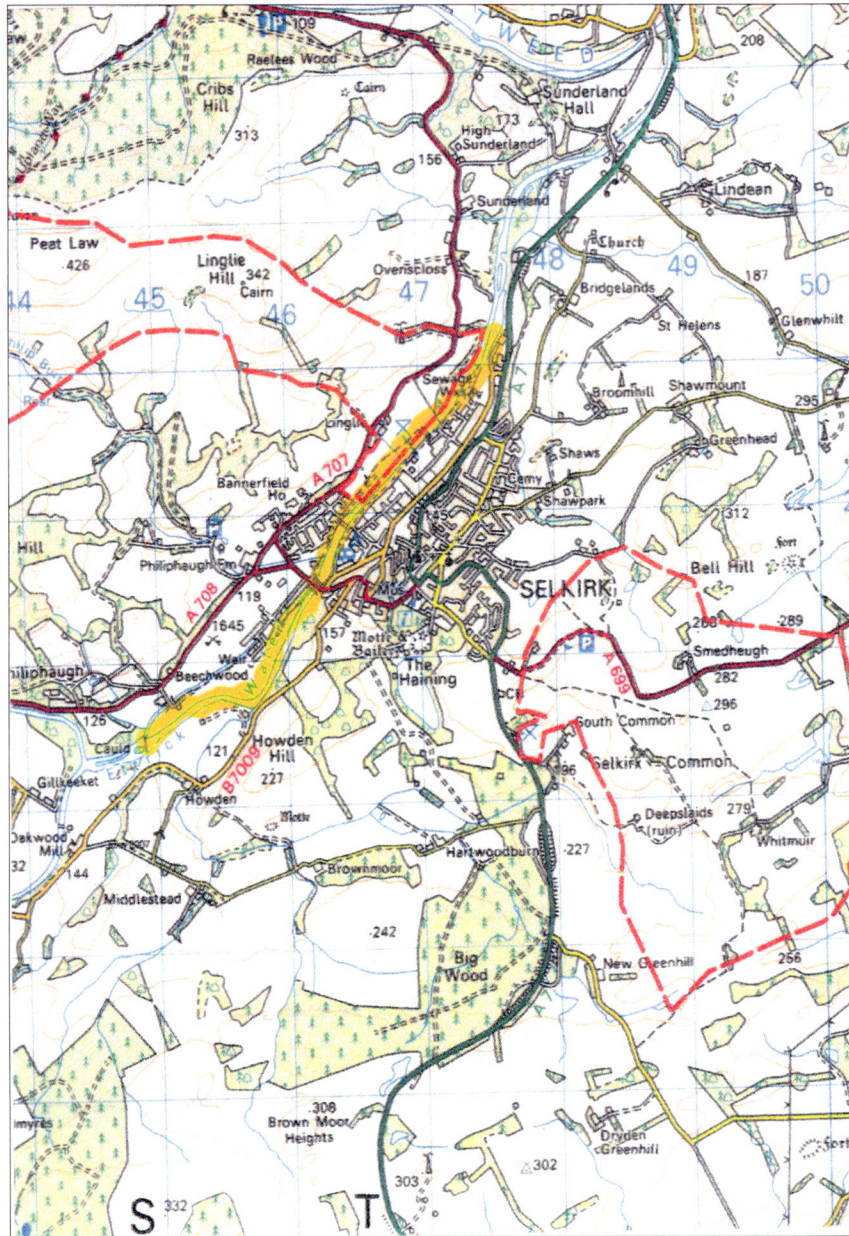

OS (1955) map showing the extent of the fishing lease of the fishing rights claimed by the Crown and for which the SAA paid a lease (marked yellow). Total is 5 miles including both banks.

What we thought

By the late 20th century, however, it was felt very keenly amongst the fishermen that what had started in 1912 as a nominal and reluctantly given payment to the Crown Estates of a £1 per annum leasing charge, which had become an agreed £5 per annum in 1914, had, over the years, increased to become £85 by 1992. This was manageable but by 2003 it had become £4,700 and was deemed unacceptable. The SAA had never had a say or taken part in any negotiations over the increases and no reason was ever given to us for the huge rises in the lease.

Throughout the 55 or so years the SAA had been leasing the fishing, the association had voluntarily administered, policed and controlled the leased fishing on the Ettrick during the 19th and 20th centuries without payment or recognition. Yet the CEC still dictated the charge level of the lease without taking this into account. The 1914 lease was nominally to the Burgh Council who later passed it to the Tweed Commissioners; they in turn passed it back to the Burgh Council who, in 1968, swiftly passed it on to the SAA. These were simply administrative steps and made no difference to the actual management of the fishings and made no difference to whom the lease money was paid. The SAA had always paid the lease, dutifully and on time.

The anglers felt their uninterrupted stewardship of the fishings was neither appreciated nor in any way recognised by the CEC and that their unpaid work was not reflected in the level of the leasing charges. The rapacious increases of charges by the CEC in the late 20th century were demanded with the accompaniment by the CEC of a verbal threat to withdraw the permission to fish the Ettrick if the SAA faltered in payment.

By now the annual SAA subscription had become unaffordable to some older association members, some of whom had resigned because of this fact. Some other members were inspired to do some checking to see if the Crown was being entirely correct about all the rights they claimed to possess. We did not trust their high-handedness and superior demeanour and felt their charges were out of control. David Mitchell, the secretary of the SAA, had himself experienced that when he or anyone else in the past had objected to the increase in lease charges, the response from the CEC representative on several occasions had been that they would simply cancel the SAA lease and advertise for another lessee on the open market. He and other SAA secretaries had tried to protest but failed. There was never anything written down about these verbal threats, so no written evidence can be shown. The anglers were clear that they did not want some outside body to gain the right to organise the fishing and fish in what they believed was their water which they had been doing for a very long time. This was seen to be a form of unfair coercion and was thoroughly resented but on several occasions the SAA reluctantly felt forced to acquiesce. So they kept on paying.

Opposite

Schematic map of the Ettrick where it runs through Selkirk showing beats. Note that the extent of the Crowns claim is less than the extent of Philiphaugh's beat. An HMW mistake!

We only realised the importance of this much later. Leased to Selkirk: Burgh's stretch 3 miles; Philiphaugh's, 2 miles; Haining's, ½ mile.

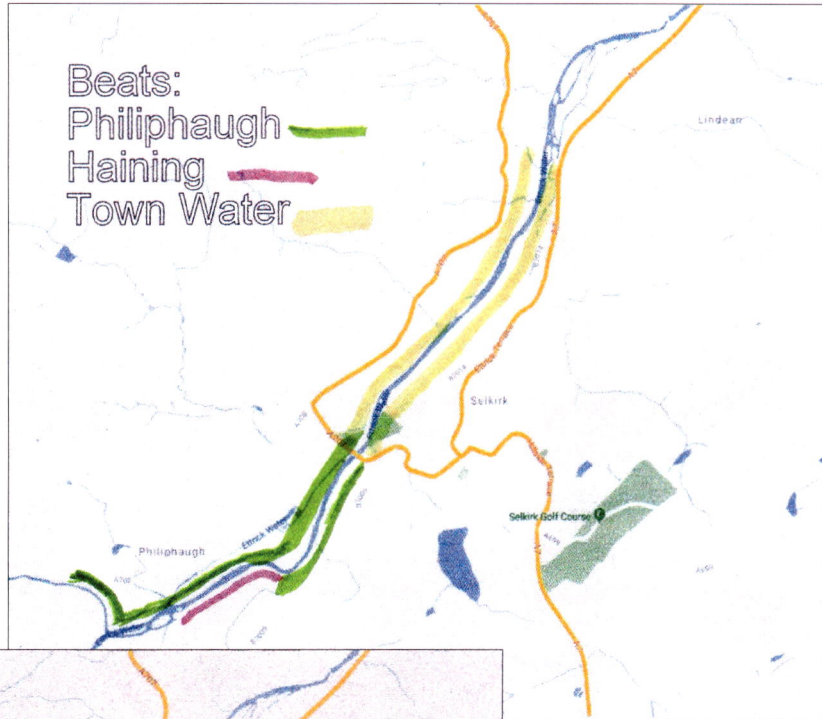

Beats:
Philiphaugh
Haining
Town Water

Extent of Crown
Estates Claim

23

The campaign starts

To start with, we needed to look at all the surviving records and old documents to see what we could find that might support our cause.

The collation and analysis of the existing charters was undertaken between 1989 and 1992 by the late David Neate, a lifelong but latterly a partially disabled fisherman, who lived in a house, Bridgeheugh, overlooking the Ettrick at the Eastern end of the leased stretch. This was at a point which marked the boundary of the Selkirk Town Water and the next present day downstream landowners, Ovenscloss and Sunderland Hall Estate.

Others became involved (*Ref 15*). In early 1993, Andrew Murray, then secretary of the SAA, also approached me, a community councillor and angling association member, to see if I would contribute to the research into the rights and wrongs of the CEC claim to own the Ettrick fishing rights. As an SAA member and being interested in history, I was up for the challenge.

During the subsequent 27 years of collective investigations, starting in 1989 and continuing until 2016, our efforts were punctuated by many ups and downs and three amazing strokes of good fortune, each of which will be described in detail later. They served to elevate our search onto an unbelievable and almost supernatural plane and provided conclusive proof that we had been right all along. The Crown had never actually owned the rights they were claiming, had been continuously claiming since 1912, and had been charging rent for them.

This is how the story unfolded.

The history of the war against superior odds

The reaction of Selkirk Burgh Council
(Extracted and condensed from Selkirk Burgh Council minutes; See Appendix C.)

In 1910 the Commissioners for HM Woods, Forests and Land Revenues (HMW), wrote to ask Selkirk Burgh Council "on what basis they exercised the salmon fishing rights" and, after lengthy correspondence which continued into 1912, claimed to own the rights for the Crown. The letter was largely identical to the one sent to Philiphaugh Estate. *(Appendix A)*

The Burgh Council, judging by the contemporary minutes, were very upset and strove to refute the Crown's claim of ownership of the Burgh's rights.

A Council minute from the time records that Thomas Craig Brown, (a councillor, a prominent textile mill owner and an acknowledged historian - the author of the 1886 'History of Selkirkshire')*, was commissioned to examine old charters to see if he could find evidence of Burgh ownership of the fishing rights.

Craig Brown's trawl had produced no specific evidence and he reported that to the Council. The local authority (Selkirk Burgh Council), also searched all of the ancient Selkirk records and consulted widely, hoping to discover documents confirming ownership. They too failed to find anything useful to support their belief in their ancient right.

---

* The 'History of Selkirkshire' book was in two volumes and totalled 1000 pages of virtually all that had ever been recorded and preserved of Selkirk's and Selkirkshire's documented history. Each episode was carefully referenced giving its origins and as a researcher Thomas Craig Brown was irreplaceable. The council was fortunate to be able to seek his help. Since 1886 there have been some amendments advocated for it in the light of more recent knowledge and a subsequent "New History" edited by John M Gilbert called 'Flower of the Forest' was published in 1984 updating the history. Another window was opened into ancient Selkirk by the revelation of Protocol Books from 1511 to 1547, which were guiltily hidden by the Mason brothers. They were bakers in the town who, in 1940, intercepted over a ton of ancient documents about to be burned to prevent their possible capture or destruction by invading German troops. When discovered, the brothers thought they had acted illegally under wartime instructions, so they hid the documents in their attic. The extant surviving brother Walter only revealed their existence in the 1980s. There was however no reference to fishing rights in the documents so far translated and researched. (Ref 39)

Despite the lack of documentary evidence to support their arguments, the Council registered a protest, hoping (perhaps rather forlornly) that further research would provide it. The Council did at least have the record of a fishing grant in an old Royal Charter of 1119 and another of 1147 *(Ref 1)* (both had been transcribed before being lost) which said that the townspeople, as well as the monks of the newly established Selkirk Abbey, were permitted to fish the King's "waters around Selkirk". These rights were referred to in a preserved Burgh charter of 1536 from James V *(Ref 13)*. These precious centuries-old charters were thought to provide sufficient evidence to substantiate the town's ancient rights to fish in the Ettrick. We decided we had enough to approach the CEC with.

HMW in 1910 nevertheless chose to ignore the Council's case and carried on regardless in pressing their claim of ownership. Later, in 1912 , in pursuance of this, they suggested an annual leasing charge, set at £5, to be levied on the Burgh to secure the rights to fish.

Selkirk Burgh Council, while not admitting the Crown had any rights over the fishings, acknowledged only that the Crown had staked a claim. In order that the Association's traditional fishing would not be interrupted – which the Crown had threatened if no payment was made (a habitual tactic as mentioned earlier) – the Council agreed to make a payment but considered the demand for £5 was excessive.

The Burgh Council recognised the weakness of their position through having no clear charter evidence but nevertheless offered to pay half a crown per annum (two shillings and sixpence or 12½ p in today's money) for a lease until they had secured an opportunity to find grounds to refute the Crown's claim.

Eventually, when pressed in 1912, the Council agreed that a £1 leasing charge could be paid. The £1 levy was regarded as affordable, enabled uninterrupted fishing to take place and was a convenient way to settle the dispute, at least temporarily. We applaud the Council all those years ago for trying to save on public expenditure – £1 was more acceptable than £5 but 2/6d would have been even better had the HMW settled for the initial half a crown! *(Appendix C)*

26

A

at Selkirk the   day of December One thousand nine hundred and ten years In presence of one of His Majesty's Justices of the Peace for the county of Selkirk Appeared William Strang Steel of Philiphaugh in the Parish and County of Selkirk, Gentleman, who being solemnly sworn depones as follows viz.

purchased the estate of Philiphaugh which includes Harehead in the Parish and County of Selkirk with entry thereto at the term of Whitsunday 15th May 1880. These lands are held under a charter under the Great Seal in favour of Sir James Murray of Philiphaugh one of the Senators of the College of Justice in liferent and John Murray his son in fee dated 15th February 1700 and ratified in Parliament and are therein called the Barony of Philiphaugh. The subjects were conveyed to me by the previous proprietor. The lands are bounded on the south west and south sides by the rivers Ettrick and Yarrow (except a small portion thereof where the lands are on

Meanwhile, in 1911, Mr William Strang Steel, the then owner of Philiphaugh Estate with whom the Crown had also been corresponding and owner of a substantial chunk of what the Crown claimed to be theirs, had died.

Before his death he complied with HMW's wishes and instructed his lawyer to draw up an affidavit *(left and overleaf)* confirming that the Estate fished their stretch of the Ettrick during the 19th century. He passed away before he could authorise the affidavit, but it was later signed by his son and successor Samuel, and 'adopted as holograph'. The Crown duly accepted it. Mr (later in 1939, Sir) William Strang Steel inherited the estate, and his son Sir Michael Strang Steel is the present owner.

We were unaware about the affidavit until the 'Glasgow miracle'. *(See p.81)*

Decorum dictated that matters with Philiphaugh Estate by HMW were not pursued further in the short term. There seems to have been little further negotiations with them nor much with Selkirk Burgh Council during 1911. Amongst the papers unearthed in the 'Glasgow miracle' was the full text of an affidavit demanded by HMW.

B

the lands there were conveyed to, ~~and~~
the fishings in the said rivers and
their tributaries.

These rivers, ~~extend~~ from the
point marked   on the sheet
No XI N.E. of the Ordnance Survey Map
sent herewith, where the lands of Harehead
march with the grounds of the residence of
Harwood Glen also in the Parish of
Selkirk to the point marked
on sheet No XII N.W. of the said map also
sent herewith, where the lands of Philiphaugh
march with the lands of Linglie also in
the said Parish and county.

Since I purchased the estate, and
I am informed for ~~many~~ years previously
the fishings in the said rivers have been
strictly preserved from the ~~pointed~~ marked A
down to Philiphaugh Cauld which is
marked on the map, and the right of
fishing exercised only by ~~me~~ through ~~my~~
servants and others ~~who~~ having ~~my~~
permission. Fishing in the river from the said
Cauld to Linglie march has been exercised
by all and sundry but only with

C

sanction and ~~I~~ consider that we would
have been legally entitled to preserve the
lower in the same as the upper portion of
the river adjoining Philiphaugh Estate
had ~~I~~ chosen to do so.

My claim applies to the north
bank of the river except between the points
marked   C   and   D.   ~~on sheet~~
~~No XII N.W. of the said map which is~~
~~sent herewith between which points~~ the
claim applies to both sides of the river.

All which is truth as the deponent
shall answer to God.

It clearly mentions the Barony of Philiphaugh. HMW were thus aware that Philiphaugh had a barony title which HMW had acknowledged in correspondence. The Estate's fishing rights appeared therefore to have been confirmed and unassailable. Why the Crown continued to question those rights and claim them for themselves is inexplicable, but that's exactly what they did. The Glasgow paper confirmed this (see p. 81).

After reams of correspondence took place between 1910 and 1912, a summary was faithfully transcribed and recorded in the Council's minute books. The Burgh Council, while continuing to question the claims of HMW, agreed to pay the nominal £1 per annum for the fishing lease on a "temporary and experimental basis" which HMW agreed was the case. The Council also made it clear that the cash was only being handed over under duress in order to enable the anglers to continue to fish the Ettrick unmolested. They did not want the anglers to suffer harassment by Water Bailiffs acting on behalf of the Crown.

The crucial written undertaking issued by HMW was that the arrangements would only apply "**until they could investigate the true ownership**" of the rights. Despite their 'promise' HMW did not embark on any investigations. *(Appendix C; entry dated 4/3/1912)*

The real negotiations began again in earnest in 1912, dragged on without resolution in a polite if contentious manner for a couple of years before being hurriedly abandoned in 1914 immediately after the outbreak of World War I.

In a nutshell the salmon rights on the River Ettrick with which we have been concerned and which were described in the original lease and offered to Selkirk Council, included the rights on three stretches of the river. They were those belonging to Philiphaugh Estate, Selkirk Burgh and the Haining Estate.

The CEC's predecessors HMW, in a letter of 1912, claimed that, unless it could be proved otherwise, each of the river's fishing rights was 'unchartered'. HMW would therefore claim to own all three as 'regalia minora' and would charge the local authority to lease the rights from them.

As far as Philiphaugh Estate were concerned, the presentation of the affidavit signifying the Estate's use of the water for fishing, and the previous acceptance by HMW that Philiphaugh did indeed own the rights, should have been enough to settle their ownership. Nevertheless some confused correspondence took place between HMW and the Estate where HMW, having accepted Philiphaugh's ownership then tried to persuade the estate to relinquish it. The Estate subsequently never did so in several letters of which we have copies. All of which makes HMW's eventual outright claim of ownership very questionable. Either serious incompetence or serious dishonesty had taken place. (*Appendix K*)

The Burgh Council on the other hand had certainly consulted widely but found no specific title deed or charter dealing with fishing rights on the Ettrick where it runs through the town. Under statute, if fishing rights had no proven owner, or were 'unchartered' then ownership fell to the Crown as a 'regalia minora'. (Property of the Crown which the monarch can give away if he so wishes by issuing a charter). The allusion here was reference to prescriptive possession (*Appendix Q*) which had been specified but not named in the letter (*Appendix A*) to Philiphaugh Estate. It was an offer made to Philiphaugh Estate to confirm their ownership but no similar offer was recorded as having been made to Selkirk Burgh Council. HMW would appear to have been applying double standards. Why was Selkirk Burgh Council not offered the same opportunity to provide evidence of continuous use in the previous decades? The question was never asked and no explanation was ever volunteered.

During the course of the wrangle over the Burgh's Town Water, the factor (estate manager) of the Philiphaugh Estate had failed to press the legitimate ownership rights of the Estate and, as we later discovered, the proprietor of the Haining estate had, through his lawyer, written to HMW indicating he "wasn't interested" in his Estate's fishing rights either.

On learning all of this, and being ignorant of the relevant law, we presumed that the letter regarding the Haining was sufficient for the Crown legitimately to claim to own the Haining Estate's fishing rights. (*Appendix N*)

The outbreak of war in September 1914 provided HMW with a cast iron opportunity to hide bad news and forestall further argument. Within a few weeks they hastily pushed up the Selkirk fishing lease from £1 to £5 per annum and got it signed. This was a fairly considerable sum in those days.

This time the terms of the lease stated unequivocally that all of the fishing rights were the property of His Majesty. There was no mention of the disputed Philiphaugh rights while the claims of Selkirk Burgh had been quietly swept under the Crown carpet! *(See p. 25)*

The Burgh Council accepted this with little hesitation. By this time everyone's attention had been diverted toward the outbreak of hostilities with Germany so the lease was willingly signed. Both Philiphaugh Estate and Selkirk Council had maintained their beliefs in their respective ownerships. But HMW, in a very cavalier fashion, had simply ignored their representations, claimed ownership and railroaded through a leasing agreement despite their earlier pledges.

This latest agreement appeared to settle things down; HMW had declared their ownership of all the fishing rights on behalf of the Crown and had extracted a small sum from Selkirk Burgh as a leasing charge. They had issued undertakings in a bid to meet the objections raised, conceding there were protests from both Selkirk Council and from Philiphaugh Estate. The Crown gave an assurance that the arrangement was "temporary and experimental" and that the leasing charge was nominal. They would also investigate true ownership further. We have copies of all the original correspondence. The Crown's claim of ownership, at least superficially, had been acknowledged by the true owners.

Selkirk could reasonably afford the annual leasing charge of £5 (eventually negotiated down to £3) to enable fishing to continue. The Council remained aggrieved that HMW had pursued this line but in the absence of documents to refute the Crown's claim of ownership and because they had received similar assurances as those given to Philiphaugh, the Burgh Council acquiesced and had signed the lease. Throughout the intervening decades the undertakings given by HMW and its successors were never cancelled. But neither were they delivered!

So phase one of the Crown's operation was thus complete; they had succeeded in their goal of amalgamating the three individually held fishing rights. Then, by making reassuring promises to both Philiphaugh and the Selkirk Burgh Council, they had persuaded the local authority and the Estate to sign on the dotted line.

SYNOPSIS OF LEASE BETWEEN THE COMMISSIONERS OF H.M. WOODS, &c., AND THE PROVOST, MAGISTRATES AND COUNCILLORS OF THE BURGH OF SELKIRK, OF SALMON FISHING IN THE RIVER ETTRICK, DATED 14th AND 22nd SEPTEMBER, AND MINUTED IN CHANCERY 6th OCTOBER 1914.

SUBJECTS

ALL AND WHOLE the right, title and interest of His Majesty in and to the fishing for Salmon and migratory fish of the Salmon kind in the River Ettrick *ex adverso* the Burgh of Selkirk, the lands of The Haining, of Bridgeheugh, and parts of the lands of Philiphaugh in the County of Selkirk from the western boundary of the lands of The Haining to the northern boundary of the lands of Bridgeheugh, as shown coloured blue on the plan annexed and signed as relative to the lease, but declaring that the right of Fishing between the points marked D (Haining west boundary) and F (Philiphaugh Cauld) and between the mouth of the Nettly Burn, marked E, and point marked C (Bridgeheugh north boundary) extends only to fishing from the right bank of said river: declaring that the right extends solely to fishing by rod and line with the artificial fly only, and that no fishing shall be carried on for a short distance below the Philiphaugh and Selkirk Caulds, and the Council shall, at their own expense, cause posts to be driven in on the banks (the riparian owners' permission being obtained) below each Cauld at a distance of fifty yards from the level of the foot of the downstream face to mark the point where angling down-stream from each Cauld may begin, and have notice boards exhibited on the posts stating that no fishing is allowed between the posts and the Cauld; and further declaring that nothing contained in the Lease shall be held to authorise the lessees to interfere with the right of salmon fishing belonging to the Crown or its grantees *ex adverso* of other lands than those above mentioned.

DURATION.

Ten years from Martimas 1913.

RENT.

£5, payable annually at Martinmas, beginning the first payment at Martinmas 1914, for the previous season's fishing.

CONDITIONS. PERMITS TO BE ISSUED.

The Lease is granted for the benefit of residents and persons residing temporarily in the said Burgh and within a three miles radius of the Town Hall—the Council to grant permits to any residents and persons residing temporarily within the limits aforesaid who may apply for them, to fish for and take, by rod and line and artificial fly only, Salmon and migratory fish of the Salmon kind, subject to the provisions of the laws and statutes applicable to Salmon Fishings in the River Tweed, which permits shall be subject to such regulations and conditions as may from time to time be approved of by said Commissioner of Woods, and shall be at the rate of 2/6 per season and 1/- per day, unless varied with the consent of said Commissioner; and declaring that permits may be refused at the discretion of the Council, it being understood, however, that this applies only to persons who may hereafter be convicted of illegal practices in fishing or to those whom there is good reason to regard as undesirable anglers.

RETURNS TO BE MADE.

The Council are (a) to use their best endeavours to obtain from persons holding permits the numbers and weights of fish caught by them; and (b) to furnish to the Office of Woods, &c., so far as in their power to do so, yearly returns at the end of each season's fishing, of the numbers and weights of fish caught, and of the numbers of permits granted.

PROSECUTIONS.

The Council bind themselves, and power is thereby conferred on them, to take, at their own expense, such proceedings in the civil or criminal courts as they may consider necessary and practicable to prevent illegal fishing in the waters thereby let, including the two areas within which no fishing is to be carried on; to prevent persons holding permits from fishing otherwise than by means of rod and line and artificial fly only, and from fishing at all in the said two areas; and to prevent persons not holding permits from fishing by any manner in said waters; and generally to enforce compliance with the provisions of the Lease and the laws applicable to the salmon fishings thereby let.

The papers and official documents we had assembled by 2005 after considerable research revealed that, apart from the Haining, all of the rights remained with the original owners! None belonged to the Crown!

One may never know why HMW created a trap for themselves and then fell into it.

Copy of the 1914 lease to Selkirk Burgh. The lease states baldly that the Crown owns the entire rights. (Ref 14.)

The Crown Estates – who actually owns them?

There is surely a constitutional issue here worthy of scrutiny. The question to be asked is whether or not the Crown 'owns' Scotland with all the additional privileges that come with ownership. The answer may lie in our country's ancient history.

Under English law the monarch owns all of England, and English property law is based on that premise. That is not in dispute. However in Scotland where property law is different, many people believe it is the Scottish people who own Scotland as the 1320 Declaration of Arbroath asserts, referring to King Robert the Bruce:

> ....Yet if he should give up what he has begun, and agree to make us or our kingdom subject to the King of England or the English, we should exert ourselves at once to drive him out as our enemy and a subverter of his own rights and ours, and make some other man who was well able to defend us our King; for, as long as but a hundred of us remain alive, never will we on any conditions be brought under English rule....

In this letter to the Pope from representatives of the Scots People, the Declaration is taken to signify that it was accepted that not only was the land owned by the Scots people but that the King himself could be replaced by the People if he failed to act adequately on their behalf.

It has been suggested that the modern Crown Estate in Scotland was simply a property manager. The land and privileges which were claimed to be Crown property were purely in the CEC portfolio for administrative convenience.

There was also much resentment that all the income from Crown Property in Scotland was delivered to the UK Treasury and was used ostensibly to offset the costs of maintaining the monarchy. This arrangement was changed in April 2017 and now the income from the Scottish Crown Estates is delivered to the Scottish Government to be spent in Scotland.

Furthermore, in legislation passed in January 2018, an interim body mimicking the previous Crown Estate in Scotland has been graced with a view to exercising a more community orientated and sympathetic approach.

An exception to this recent rôle was the valuable piece of real estate by the name of Fort Kinnaird in Edinburgh which was deemed not to be a Scottish asset but a Crown Estate (England) asset. The Crown Estate's half share was sold in 2018 for £167.5 million. Scotland received nothing from the sale which illustrates how crown assets in Scotland can be manipulated. The new approach for the CEC to be more equitable is open to question.

The distinction between the Scottish and English parts of the previous Crown Estate was clearly demonstrated in 1999 when the newly formed Scottish Government was obliged to acquiesce to the transfer of jurisdiction of large tracts of the North Sea, previously denominated as Scottish, into English ownership.

The obscure criterion used to redefine the maritime boundary between the nations was the bizarre extension of the average orientation of the last nine miles of the River Tweed culminating in its mouth. From there an imaginary line was drawn to where it met the line internationally agreed under maritime law delineating Norwegian waters. It meets it north of Carnoustie.

The result was that England gained the income and privileges of a further 6000 square miles of formerly Scottish North Sea maritime territory along with seven oil fields. This act of blatant piracy on the high seas significantly enhanced the value of the Crown Estates in England in relation to oil and gas exploration and fishing rights. It was secretively signed off the night before the Scottish Parliament came into existence and has never been debated in either Parliament. This is not right!

However, for some reason the criteria to determine the apportionment of the border at the mouth of the Solway in the Irish Sea were not applied in the same way at the Scottish/English boundary at the mouth of the Tweed. Had a similar set of rules been used the Scottish sector would have extended in the sea well down into England!

Who were HM Woods, Forests & Land Revenues, Works and Buildings in 1910?

The principal fixer of the fishing lease to Selkirk Burgh Council and Philiphaugh Estate was Sir Edward Stafford Howard Bt. KCB DL JP. He was HMW commissioner from 1892 to 1912. A nephew of the Duke of Norfolk, he was a lawyer educated at Harrow and Cambridge University. Howard married Lady Georgina, the daughter of the Earl of Cawdor and moved in the highest echelons of Edwardian society. He sat as a Liberal MP in Cumberland before landing the top job with the Crown in Scotland.

This well connected knight of the realm was succeeded by George Leveson Gower (knighted in 1921) who pronounced his name "Loosen Gore". He was the grandson of the Duke of Sutherland and also of Earl Granville. He attended Eton and Balliol College and when an MP he became private secretary to Prime Minister Gladstone. He was related by marriage to the Bowes-Lyon family which rendered him a relative of Queen Elizabeth, the late Queen Mother.

"My dear George". Caricature of Edward Leveson-Gower by Spy published in Vanity Fair in 1886. Private Secretary to WE Gladstone

Both of these Crown commissioners were high born and therefore would not normally waste time in discussions or arguments with a far flung little council in a small Borders burgh. They were used to ordering their minions about and habitually got their own way. They demanded respect and expected to receive it.

Sir George Leveson Gower, was a Liberal MP during 1890s for Staffordshire. His grandfather, the infamous Duke of Sutherland, whose statue controversially graces the hill behind Golspie in Sutherland, is still reviled for his part in

35

the Highland Clearances. There was therefore not a family history of sympathy being afforded to indigenous Scottish communities!

It is to their credit therefore that Selkirk Town Council mustered such strong resistance against the formidable force facing them. But perhaps it was typical of the times that the establishment, and especially one studded with titles, would prevail. It was not considered normal or even good form to question authority.

Conclusion of Phase One, the Crown has achieved its aim

After the initial flurry of protests, many arguments and voluminous correspondence – all brought to an abrupt end by World War I – a summary of the outcome in 1914 was as follows:

The Selkirk Burgh water

As detailed above, the Burgh Council had eventually signed the lease under protest. The Crown still maintained they owned the rights. Selkirk still claimed ownership of the Burgh stretch. *(Appendix C)*

The Philiphaugh Estate Stretch

The Philiphaugh Estate insisted on retaining ownership of their rights which HMW had acknowledged to them, but had by 1914 acquiesced in the arrangement whereby the Crown leased the Philiphaugh rights to Selkirk Burgh while maintaining ownership. HMW had also agreed that the arrangements regarding Philiphaugh were only "temporary" and "experimental". We have a copy of the letter confirming this. *(Appendix K)*

[It was recognised and acknowledged by the Estate in 2003 that Philiphaugh's factor in 1912 had palpably failed to represent his employer's interests and had not strenuously objected to the arrangement. That was the reason that Philiphaugh had not contested the proposals from the Crown more vehemently at the time.]

36

As a minor but legally important detail, HMW defined the western boundary of Philiphaugh's claimed right and what they were claiming was theirs as terminating at Murray's Cauld. This left the Estate free to fish for salmon on a small stretch of the Ettrick beyond the Cauld and a section of the Yarrow, neither of which was included in the Crown's lease. This turned out to be a fascinating little anomaly.

As a result of a decision in the Court of Session, this turned out to be further confirmation that legally the Estate retained title to the whole fishery. At that stage, we were unaware that Philiphaugh held a barony title. It proved unnecessary later on to press this point but it emphasised that the Philiphaugh Estate had not surrendered their title to the fishings under Scots Law and continued to own the title even though the Crown claimed to own it. Under the existing Scots law, the CE simply **could not own** the rights to Philiphaugh fishings. We were delighted to be able to confirm this after due research.* *(Ref 8)*

Green's Encyclopedia of the Law of Scotland, 2nd. Ed., 1911, Vol VI reports:
Lovat (1880) "…it was held that possession of salmon-fishings on a barony title in certain parts of a river was sufficient to prescribe the right on the whole river…".

The Haining Estate Stretch

(These conclusions were based on the letter later discovered in the Glasgow Papers and reproduced at Appendix N)

The Haining Estate owner had voluntarily intimated to HMW that he surrendered his Estate's interest in the fishing rights and had written via a Melrose lawyer (James Curle, the renowned archaeologist, first reporter and discoverer of the misplaced Roman Fort of Trimontium) that "he had no interest in the salmon fishing". *(Appendix N)*

HMW had, for their own convenience, taken that to mean that they could adopt the ownership even although no legally binding disposition had taken place. It is a minor legal point that while the title remained with the Estate, the Crown was simply wrong in law by claiming Regalia Minora* rights and assuming ownership. This actually constituted another act of property misappropriation by HMW!

The SAA and Selkirk Burgh Council wrongly assumed the HMW claim to the Haining fishing rights had been established so they did not consider challenging that claim. It is easy to see now that HMW were simply making false claims of ownership for the sake of expediency and for their own advantage.

That was how the arrangements remained until 1924 when HM Woods, Forests and Land Revenues became the Crown Estates Commission, (hereinafter CEC, the Crown or Crown Estate) This change in the organisation of the Crown Estates did not affect the lease of the fishing to SAA at all.

Regalia Minora:

Regalia Minora are the inherited properties of the monarch within a defined group over which he/she can retain ownership or bestow at will on whomsoever he/she chooses. Salmon fishing rights, rights to run ferries and the ownership of the foreshore between high and low water tidal marks are examples. But there is a condition; unless the monarch-approved owner exercises his/her rights, such as fishing for salmon where rights have been granted by charter, the property automatically reverts to the Crown. Also, where no charter exists conferring a crown right on a specific recipient, the Crown can declare such a right 'unchartered' and claim ownership under the terms of the 'Regalia Minora'. So it was with all the fishing rights that the SAA enjoyed on the Ettrick; the CEC (HMW) had initially declared them all unchartered in 1910 and in their opinion they therefore belonged to the Crown.

Phase II

How the arrangement worked for most of the 20th Century

1914 until 1980s

After the early wrangles over ownership, the revised fishing arrangements were in place with the SAA continuing to pay the annual leasing charge.

During this period the Angling Association agreed to monitor, police and control the fishing of the leased Ettrick Water. Behind the scenes, the overall administrative responsibility passed in turn from the Burgh Council to the Tweed Commissioners and back to the local authority before ending up with the SAA.

Sixty tickets were issued annually by the Association - usually to the previous years' members, while any vacancies were filled on a first come, first served basis.

This arrangement was acceptable to both the Angling Association (who had not asked for any remuneration for their effort in controlling the fishing) and the Crown Estate until the 1980s. The Crown Estates had been imposing ever increasing annual leasing sums on the small Selkirk and District Angling Association who, until then, had been willingly paying the sums demanded. In 1992, the leasing charge stood at £85 which it had been for some years, and that was, at the time, deemed reasonable.

Beyond the 1980s

In 1993 there was a sea change in the 80-year-old arrangements wholly due to a new policy of the Crown Estates to enhance revenue to the CEC.

In previous years the cost of the lease had increased gradually in regular steps. In 1993 the leasing charge shot up from £85 to £600 and by 2003 it had rocketed to £4,000.

When VAT was added to the bill the demand on the Angling Association was close to an eye-watering £5,000.

These charges could no longer be described as nominal as they had been when the Crown seized control in 1912-14. We were led to believe the Crown Estates had been instructed to maximise their income and that would include leasing charges for fishing rights. However, this level of exorbitant profiteering was condemned in Selkirk, and some of us started to look into the Crown Estate's justification for the price rises.

We immediately encountered the form of pressure which had been employed in the past by the Crown Estate. They warned – nay verbally threatened – that if the SAA chose not to pay the increased lease charges, the lease would be advertised on the open market and the salmon fishing could possibly be lost to Selkirk people. We have no written record of these threats, only actual witnesses.

To avoid risking such a loss the SAA paid up grudgingly. But this fired up members of the Association to question whether the Crown actually owned the rights they claimed to own. And could that asserted claim to ownership be challenged, in court if necessary? The SAA had squirrelled away substantial funds to allow a court battle to be afforded if it proved necessary.

The SAA took stock.

A summary so far

At various stages during our challenge – and at the 1912 outset when the fishing rights were appropriated – the representatives and predecessors of what is now The Crown Estates Commission had issued undertakings and made assertions nearly all of which were eventually found to be false or misleading.

Examples are, that HMW would examine ownership, leasing charges would be nominal, that the fishing rights were unchartered, and that all arrangements would be temporary and experimental. None of these undertakings or guarantees were fulfilled.

In more recent years it appeared the CEC was deliberately prolonging negotiations in order to extract additional lease money out of the Selkirk and District Angling Association (SAA). They were maximising their income in accordance with their policies but ignoring past agreements and undertakings and refusing to listen to any protest. This will be alluded to later.

Our research had revealed that ever since descending on Selkirk's waters, the CEC had made no effort at all to establish the true ownership of the fishing rights which had been the undertaking given in 1914.

By this time – the 1990s – the SAA felt that the so-called experiment to which the CEC had agreed had run its course so the deal should be called off.

The exorbitant leasing charge of £4,000 plus VAT eventually demanded meant that the previously acceptable arrangement which allowed senior citizens and others to participate in their chosen sport had ceased to exist. The nominal cost of fishing was no longer nominal!

Before undertaking our research project into the Crown Estate's actions we needed to become familiar with the legislation which governs salmon fishing in Scotland. We needed to learn a lot more about the law.

The law governing salmon fishing

From mediaeval times salmon fishing rights had been considered to be of great significance, meriting a legal framework and legal protection along the lines of property ownership but nominally separated from it and they should be clearly stated on the title deeds.

Salmon fishing rights are inherently the property of the Crown under statutes detailing Crown 'Regalia Minora' *(see description p38)*. The Crown may have granted the rights by charter specifically to an individual or as part of a barony, but they reverted to the Crown if they were unclaimed and unused for a period of time.

This is the prescriptive possession* route to ownership under property law.

Salmon rights were applied in property law in the same way as land or buildings and had to be specified and included when a land transaction took place. Alternatively they had to be separately granted outwith a transfer of land title. This was the time-honoured mechanism where rights to fish for salmon in a river were transferred from one owner to another. *(Appendix Q)*

An enquiry to the late Brian Gilmour, a lawyer in the town in March 1993, revealed that from the definitive text book on the law:

> *"There are three ways that fishing rights can be owned as property:*
>
> a) *As a direct grant; but 'fishings' along with pertinents (buildings, land orchards etc.) has been accepted as a valid title. (Sinclair 1867 & McCulloch 1874) or;*
>
> b) *As a separate grant of fishings where previously granted if prescriptive possession* is proven. or;*
>
> c) *By the prescriptive possession of salmon fishings by the holder of a barony title with or without fishings.*
>
> *And: "possession for twenty years is probably sufficient to establish prescription"*
>
> (Extracted from Green's Encyclopedia of the Law of Scotland, 2nd. Ed., 1911, Vol VI)

A word about Charters

Most charters granted prior to the 18th century were written in Latin. A fishing right title is enhanced if the original charter contains a grant in Latin of fishing, where it says either 'cum piscationibus' or 'piscariis'. From previous court decisions however, it was not always necessary to specifically mention 'fishings' as they could sometimes be assumed to accompany a charter.

<u>Stair Memorial Encyclopedia, 1990, Vol 11</u>. Confirms the above, and specifically mentions that the use of 'piscariis' in a title deed generally means salmon fishing as opposed to other river fish. *(Ref 8 & Ref 17)*

> ** 'Prescription' in a legal context is a way of establishing ownership to a property or a right and was fixed at 20 years throughout most of the 20th century. Thus if you used an unclaimed/unowned property for 20 years and no-one else could produce evidence of ownership, you could claim it was yours. This works for tangible property such as land, housing etc and crucially fishing rights. Conversely, if you failed to use a 'right' granted from the Crown for 20 years such as salmon fishing, it could revert to becoming property of the Crown again. (This had originally been 40 years) A 'habile'* title, if one was discovered, would displace prescription as the foundation of ownership.*

Trout fishing or fish <u>not</u> "of the salmon kind" were classed as owned by the owner of a loch or riverbank and needed no separate property conveyance. When a property was conveyed to someone else, the trout fishing went along with the land without needing to be specified.

Note: *Originally in 1993 we were unaware that Philiphaugh was a barony and were developing a case for the Selkirk Town Water alone solely on the basis of the Burgh Charter of 1535/6 and the 12th century charters to the monks of Selkirk Abbey. They each mentioned the rights of the monks to fish in the King's "waters around Selkirk" along with "my people" ie. the inhabitants of Selkirk. We considered this was our proof by charter.*

---

*'habile' is an old word and is defined as something being legally competent in Scots law since at least the 15th century.

The first breakthrough

The Edinburgh Miracle

The discovery of a charter: King James VI's unrecognised Manuscript of 1615 *(Ref 10)*

Was Lady Luck starting to take an interest in us? In September 2000 there was an auction sale of books and manuscripts in Edinburgh which I happened to attend because I was selling a few volumes of my own. While browsing some of the items before they went under the hammer I spotted six old manuscripts in one lot in the documents and manuscripts section. Intriguingly some of the documents related to Selkirk. They were lying on a bench all bound together protected in clear plastic pockets. The lot was entitled 'Scottish 17th Century Manuscripts'. The detailed catalogue description was:

a) [Murray, of Philiphaugh] A Marriage certificate dated 1606.

b) A Certificate of Discharge from Walter Scott claiming back land from Murray of Philiphaugh; 1629.

c) Letters to a Sheriff informing him of a land transaction between Murray of Elibank, and Murray of Philiphaugh 1615.

d), e) & f) three other land registry documents relating to Lanark and Kilbride and of no importance to Selkirk. One was from 1579.

It was because three of them mentioned Selkirk and Philiphaugh that I thought they were worth bidding for because of historical interest, and I acquired them successfully. There was no clue at that stage to make me believe they had anything to do with fishing.

When the six documents were brought home to Selkirk for closer scrutiny we saw they consisted of a mixture of letters or deeds handwritten in either old Scots or Latin. This was normal in documents of the period – from the late 14th century Scots was used in less

44

formal documents, Latin being reserved for the more formal and important ones and Latin continued to be used for this purpose and on Royal Charters until the 18th century.

Of the six manuscripts, only one – the "Letters to a Sheriff" – was written in Latin. The rest were in Scots but apart from the old Scots language used, the handwriting was also very difficult to decipher to an untrained eye.

Manuscript 'c', the "Letters to a Sheriff", which required both deciphering and translation, turned out to be the golden ticket – like the one handed to Charlie Bucket in Roald Dahl's Willie Wonka and the Chocolate Factory. The Latin text in this manuscript seemed even at first glance the most interesting. The auction house had stated it was simply a land transaction in 1615 between Sir John Murray of Philiphaugh and Lord Gideon Murray of Elibank. Had they looked more closely they would have discovered that, near the end, it was much more!

The original vellum or parchment manuscript was beautifully written in secretary hand and was taken to the palaeographer Teresa Maley who had recently deciphered the 16th century documents collection known as the Walter Mason Papers discovered in Selkirk. She lived locally and was happy to take a look at our recently acquired manuscript. At the time she was a member of The Royal Burgh of Selkirk and District Community Council.

Teresa Maley, after reading the manuscript and simultaneously translating it from the Latin, soon declared "This is a Barony Charter making John Murray the Baron of Philiphaugh". For us in the campaign group it was a eureka moment!

The significance of it was this: one of the ways in which someone could own fishing rights, as mentioned above, was if the individual concerned possessed a barony. Barony rights usually stated that all the land, buildings, mills etc. were part of the monarch's gift of a barony and that fishing, where relevant, was part of the deal.

If it was included, the latin word 'piscariis' or 'piscationibus' was proof of the inclusion although the absence did not necessarily exclude fishing. Trout fishings, as explained above, were not separately mentioned in title deeds or charters. Salmon rights were considered more important and merited separate mention in deeds of ownership or transfer so it was important to seek the mention of fishings in the Philiphaugh charter.

('Green's Encyclopaedia states also that simple references to 'fishings' can mean salmon fishings. Ref. 8)

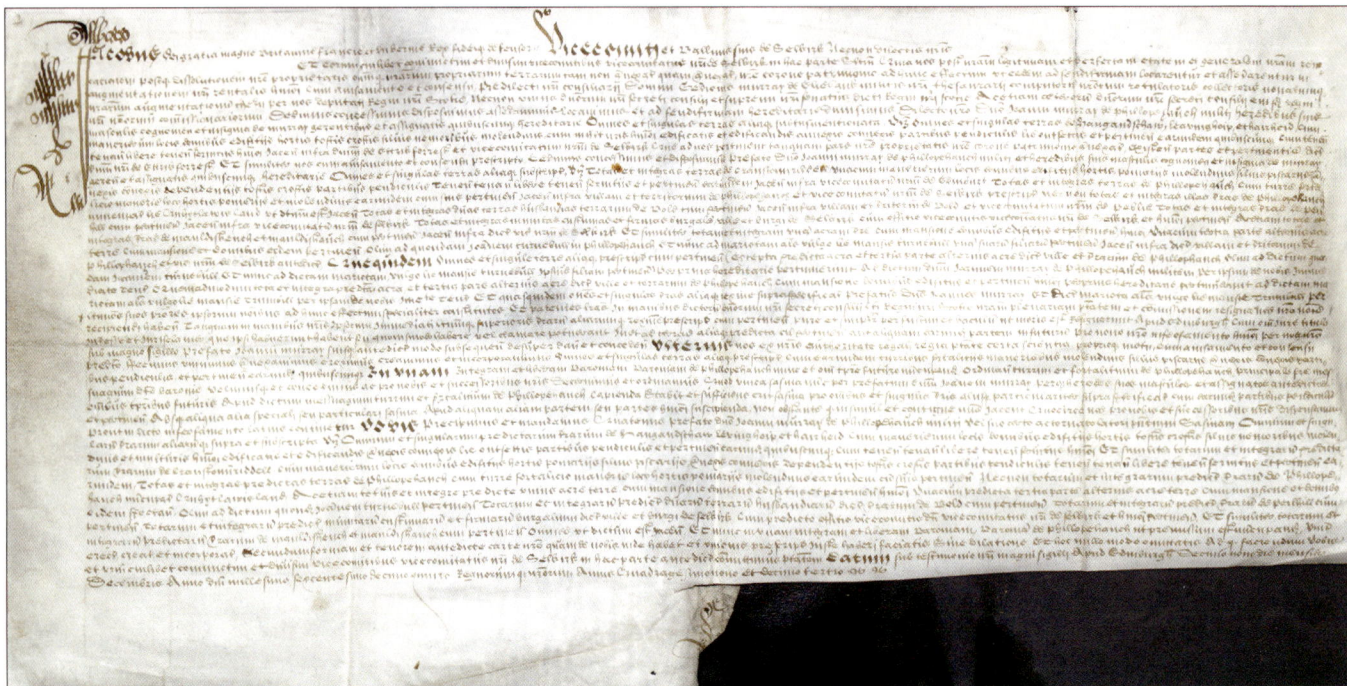

The original charter from King James VI. 1615

It starts; ***Jacobus dei gratia magne brittanie et francie et hibernie rex fidelque…***

ie. ***James, by the grace of God, King of Great Britain, France and Ireland and Defender of the Faith…***

About 2/3 of the way down, it grants the barony to John Murray.

The discovered manuscript: what it actually said

In 1615, Sir Gideon Murray was King James VI's treasurer and controller of the Royal Purse. He was also styled Lord Elibank in his role as a law lord. The charter written in that year, clearly stated that besides wishing to honour Sir John Murray of Philiphaugh, the King wished to enhance his own income by elevating The Philiphaugh Estate into a barony which could then be expected to contribute to his coffers. Sir Gideon Murray approved the king's proposal.

When the manuscript came up for sale, the auction house in Edinburgh had not realised that the document was a Royal Charter. They were probably misled by the absence of a royal signature and seal which someone had cut off in the past. They also failed to read beyond the first few paragraphs to where the barony grant was outlined.

The auction house had completely got the wrong end of the stick. Their note accompanying the manuscript said:

> # Elibank Castle
>
> [see RCAMS 'County of Selkirk' No 13, p 36]
> ..... 'This castle was presumably built by Sir Gideon Murray of Glenpoit, who acquired Elibank from John Liddell of Halkerstone in 1594-95. This Gideon Murray, 3rd son of Andrew Murray of Blackbarony, entered the ministry, became chamberlain and guardian to his relative, Sir Walter Scott of Buccleuch, was knighted by James VI in 1605, became a member of the Privy Council in 1610, Treasurer Depute two years later and a Lord of Session in 1613. In 1621 he fell from favour and died a few months later. In 1722 the castle was already in ruin.
> ..... see letter from Sir Walter Scott to Miss Seward, June 29, 1802 ....., on his ancestor, Sir William Scott .... son of Wat Scott of Harden ...about his being caught by Sir Gideon, raiding at Elibank, & made to marry Gideon's daughter ... 'Meikle-mouthed Meg'.

We had to check that the charter contained the reference to fishings. Thus there were two hurdles to overcome in understanding the charter and finding the relevant Latin phrases in it. First we had to interpret the meaning from the strange form of handwriting used in those times and second we needed to translate the mediaeval Latin used in framing the text and identify the reference to fishings. There was also frequent use of a form of legal shorthand in Latin which was very confusing.

A transcription followed by an approximate translation was shown to Teresa Maley. She corrected the mistakes and read the charter as if it had been written in modern English. The important part of the charter from our point of view was quickly identified – about two-thirds of the way down was written

> *"…fecimus annexaminus, ereximus creavimus et incorporavimus omnes et singulas aliaque prescriptis cum earundem turribus fortaliciis manieribus molendinis silvis* **piscariis** *et nexis connexis partibus pendiculis et pertinentis earundem quibuscunque* **in unam integram et liberam** *Baroniam…"*

 …which translates as

> *"We make over, annex, erect, create and incorporate all and whole of those things previously written down with their towers, fortalices, manors, mills, woods,* **fishings** *and together with the dependant parts connected thereto,* **In one whole** *and free barony"*

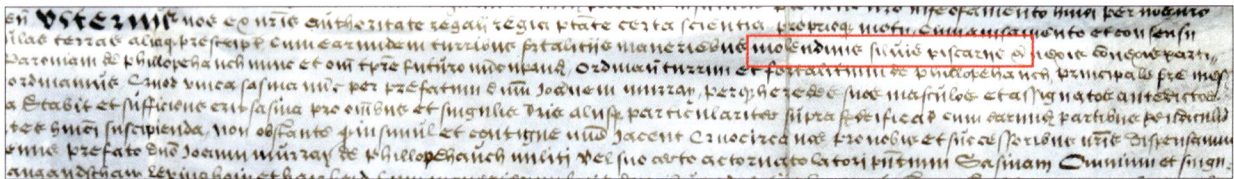

Detail from the 1615 Charter (outlined in red) saying "…molendiniis silvis piscariis" – "…mills, woods, fishings"

This confirmed that the ownership of fishing rights accompanied this barony charter to Sir John Murray of Philiphaugh as the magic word 'piscariis' had been specifically mentioned.

So we now had concrete evidence that Philiphaugh Estate owned the fishings in the river bordering on the Estate in 1615, and we had proof from the original charter saying just that.

48

A painstaking trawl through the Register of Sasines, covering the period up until the Steel family bought the estate in 1890, was then undertaken to confirm that the fishing rights had been disponed (legally sold) along with the barony and had not been sold off separately. After a lengthy search there was no record of the ownership of the fishings having been disposed of in the 265 years since the charter was written.

The Book of the Great Seal was consulted and showed that a simple search by the CEC's predecessors would have revealed the barony title to them as it did to us. The barony title was confirmed by an act of 1700. So we knew that the Commission had not carried out such a search between 1912 and 1914. They simply hadn't bothered. No attempt to clarify ownership had been undertaken by HMW which was in direct breach of HMW's written promise to do so when it commandeered the Selkirk river fishings. From the records of land and property sales recorded in the Sasines of Selkirkshire, the fishing rights had not been sold off between 1615 and 1880. We had also verified the veracity of the 1615 charter by the fact that it had been ratified by an act of Parliament.

The timeline, the results of the researches and the conclusions we reached before presenting our case to the Commission are catalogued below:

Chronology relating to Contesting the Crown's Claim of ownership

**The main relevant events and charters prior to the
Crown's Claim in 1910.**

The Selkirk part:

12TH CENTURY

In a charter of **1119 AD** establishing an abbey in Selkirk and granting land to accompany the founding of it, there is the reference of the entitlement to fish by the monks and "by my people of Selkirk…my waters about Selkirk". The charter had been granted by David 1, when he was still Earl David. He repeated this charter in 1147 and it was later confirmed by Malcolm IV, in 1159. This last charter has survived. The two earlier charters were lost but the text had been copied by the monks and the transcripts had survived. *(Ref 1)*

The perfidious Douglases *(Appendix D)*

Between 1306 and 1747 Selkirk itself was frequently the subject of barony grants, mainly to the Douglas family. The Douglases changed sides so often, losing and regaining the barony every time, that many of those charters have survived. Later Selkirk Burgh (a burgh from at least 1138) had itself replaced the Douglases and administered the barony unopposed from 1747 when George III abolished the traditional rights of barons. The barony charters to the Douglas family specified 'fishings' (piscariis) as part of the barony grant in some of the surviving charters. Selkirk Burgh thus inherited the fishing rights that had been part of the original barony and owned them from 1747. *(See Appendix D for details of the Selkirk Barony.)*

The fact that Selkirk had been a barony for several hundred years and had had possession of the fishing rights attached to the barony, was unknown to us at the time of our subsequent submitting our Adverse Claim to the CEC. *(p. 58)*

What Selkirk once had

Lost Charters

Selkirk had unfortunately lost much of the Burgh's possessions (all charters, documents, town regalia etc.) when a raiding party in 1418 headed by Sir Robert d'Umphraville, Governor of Berwick, had sacked the Burgh. It is assumed that in the process he destroyed all the old documents. Thus there were no relevant ancient charters to present to the CEC. *(Ref 1, Charters)*

However, King James V re-granted a charter of Burgh rights "to the community of

Selkirk" in 1535/6 to replace the previously lost charters and any lost after Flodden. Where burgh's rights are mentioned elsewhere in ancient documents they would normally, included any fishings, although the charter to Selkirk unfortunately does not specifically mention this. These various charters were nevertheless going to be the basis of the claim of title in respect of the fishing rights on the 'Town Water' of Selkirk because they did once exist and their contents were known and recorded. *(Ref 13)*

In **1668** The Laird of Haining claimed entitlement to pasturage on Selkirk Common in an action in the Court of Session. The Burgh had tried to deny him access for his animals on the grounds that he did not have grazing rights. The Burgh lost and Haining won but the action emphatically inter alia (among other things) confirmed that Selkirk was indeed a barony with concomitant barony rights. However, because the Haining owner's case was not about fishing rights it could not be used in support of Selkirk's claim to the fishing.

The status of Selkirk as a barony was confirmed. *(Ref 27; Appendices D & G)*

From **1802 to 1910** The Burgh administered the fishing of the Town Water. Management was eventually delegated to the SAA who upheld the fishing laws and let out the fishings to its members. The 1802 burgh minute specifically says "reserving burgess rights to fish". This was further support for the Burgh having possession of the fishing rights.

Additional Evidence

Besides the original charters and evidence of a barony, we had discovered a number of historical references which supported the case to assert that Selkirk had never lost its fishing rights. *(Ref 2,3,5; Appendices D & G)*

They were:

Act of King Charles II 1681 – Book of the Great Seal: VIII, pp. 419-428

Selkirk lost 88% of its Common Good Land:

In **1681** Selkirk 'commontie' was broken up and shared out among aggressive and rapacious local landowners under an act of Parliament. The excuse for breaking up and redistributing Selkirk's property was to avoid further violent disputes between the townsfolk and surrounding landowners who coveted the land owned by Selkirk and had engineered the disharmony. Selkirk's valuable inheritance was being predated upon by titled and powerful neighbours and was pretty powerless to assert and protect its ancient rights.

A Selkirk provost now known as 'Muthag' but probably really called 'MacHaig' was murdered in a dispute over Burgh land boundaries which the provost was trying to defend. Eventually an arbitration committee was set up with both landowner and Burgh representatives charged to come to a decision over land boundaries before a panel of judges.

Nearly all of the surrounding landowners received a portion of the spoils. As a result, Selkirk's 'commontie' was reduced from about 11,200 acres of mixed hill and fertile arable land to 1300 acres of mainly rough hill pasture.* The purpose of this was said "to avert further conflict" which had affected the Burgh for decades and at times had resulted in physical violence. The real purpose was to take possession of the inheritance of the Burgh inhabitants and give it to private landowners. With most of their property gone, the Selkirk folk had little to defend and peace did indeed result.

After due deliberation, which was anything but impartial, Selkirk ended up losing much of its best common land to achieve peace. The Haining Estate acquired a small portion of land abutting the Ettrick.

---

*The fully armed menfolk traditionally had to "ride the marches" to signify and preserve the Burgh's ownership and were frequently assaulted by landowners' gangs claiming rights on Burgh land. This is now commemorated by the annual Selkirk Common Riding which today in June follows a route round the remaining North Common Burgh property.

The town councillors, who were supposedly representing Selkirk's interests on the arbitration committee and ostensibly on behalf of the people of Selkirk, were signatories to the arbitration act and were also granted land. It is difficult to avoid concluding that the Selkirk representatives were acting in their own interests and not in the interests of the Burgh folk.

Selkirk still to this day retains its 1300 acres of common land, mostly rough hill pasture, which is only 12% of what it once possessed! The best land was claimed and had been given to surrounding landowners, the biggest share going to the Earl of Roxburgh. He acquired most of the Selkirk South Common and land as far as Bowden. Fishing rights were not in dispute so this episode of destruction of the commonty was of no help to our case. It does, however, illustrate very well the predatory behaviour of the times and the greed of some councillors and landowners alike. *(Ref 4 & 7)*

Philiphaugh Estate

In **1615** the Philiphaugh barony with fishings was created and a charter granted to the Murray family by King James VI. This was the charter found at the auction sale in Edinburgh illustrating that between 1615 and 1870 fishing was conducted without hindrance on the Philiphaugh stretch of water. The importance of this is described in detail above. The Estate owned the fishing. *(Ref 10)*

The Haining Estate

In **1870** a deed of entail had been drawn up relating to the inherited properties of the Haining Estate, including the specific mention of fishing. The purpose of this obscure legal measure (no longer practiced) was to secure inheritance to named persons within the family who owned the Haining Estate and legally prevent the breaking up of the Estate's assets. The importance to us was that it specifically mentioned the fishing and meant salmon fishing. The significance of this document will be explained later but we knew nothing about it at the time. We had not researched the background of the Haining Estate fishing believing the rights to be securely held by the Crown. As the Haining was barely mentioned in the correspondence we had unearthed, we did not mention it ourselves in the forlorn hope that the Crown was unaware that it was part of the lease.

 The successful 1912 attempt by the Crown Estates to take possession of the fishing rights was a grim reminder of the theft of Burgh property perpetrated in 1681!

The timeline thereafter, the results of the researches and the conclusions we reached in assembling our case against the Crown are set out below.

1910 to 2003 summary of events in diary form

In **1910** It all began when HMW asked Selkirk Burgh Council if it was they who owned the fishing rights. A similar enquiry was directed at Philiphaugh Estate, and we later obtained the relevant correspondence. *(Appendix A)*

In **1911** Mr William Strang Steel died. His son, Samuel, inherited. Correspondence ceased during 1911, but during **1912** several significant things happened:

a) HMW acknowledged Philiphaugh's fishing rights. *(Appendix K)*

b) Prof. Pringle-Pattison (Haining owner) renounced his interest in fishing rights of the Haining Estate. *(Appendix N)*

c) HMW state that their aim was to put together a worthwhile fishing stretch to lease to Selkirk Burgh and thereby control it, control poaching and lessen pollution.

d) HMW pledged that all the arrangements were "temporary and experimental" and in a written assurance to Selkirk Burgh (which was noted in council minutes) that leasing charges were to be "nominal, temporary and experimental". *(Appendices M & C)*

e) HMW, despite acknowledging Philiphaugh's ownership, nevertheless claimed to own all the fishing rights, from the Philiphaugh (Murray's) Cauld to Bridgeheugh. *(See p. 31. Ref 14)*

f) HMW issued a lease to Selkirk Burgh for £5 per annum. Selkirk initially offered only 2/6d, but then ultimately settled on £1. Selkirk Burgh, unable to find documentary proof of its ownership, while reserving its belief in its rights, accepted the arrangements in view of the nominal nature of the leasing charge but only as far as recognising that the Crown had made a claim, not that it was a valid one. *(Appendix C)*

g) Philiphaugh Estate also acquiesced, but reserved its fishing rights. *(Appendix K)*

In **1914** Selkirk entered into a ten year lease with HMW at £5 per annum (backdated to Martinmas 1913) in which it again states that the Crown owns all the salmon fishing rights (Murray's Cauld to Bridgeheugh). The lease was hurriedly arranged and signed within six weeks of WWI breaking out. *(Appendix C; Ref 14)*

In **1924** HMW becomes Crown Estates.

In **1947** River Tweed Commission (RTC) took over the lease from Selkirk Burgh by mutual agreement.

In **1968** the RTC transferred the lease to Selkirk and District Angling Association on the recommendation of the Burgh Council. The lease was now for £50 per annum.

In **1989** David Neate (DN) wrote to Ettrick and Lauderdale District Council (E&LDC) to enquire if there are any Selkirk Burgh records regarding ownership of the fishing rights on the Town Water. The reply he got from E&LDC asserted that their view was that the Crown owned the rights. There was nothing in the archives suggesting otherwise since 1914 when "…the Crown who had right to the Salmon Fishings…" said E&LDC.

In **1992 (July)** David Neate and Colin Cairney (Secy. SAA) continue questioning the ownership but E&LDC decline to take the matter further. The Crown Estates Commission sent the SAA a letter raising the lease from £85 to £600 per annum then rising by £100 annually from 1993 onwards. Following even larger increases, the lease reached £1000 in 1997, £1250 in 2002 & £4000 pa from 2003 onwards. Each fee had VAT added.

In **1993** Drew Murray (late Secy. of S&DAA) approached me, Lindsay Neil (LDN), who as a result undertook to do further research based on DN's earlier findings.

In **1993/4** LDN's research assisted by Brian Gilmour and others confirms that a case could be made to contest the CEC's ownership of Burgh fishing rights.

In **1994** the SAA was reluctant to embark on what might be a possibly expensive legal case and preferred to pay the increased leasing charge (£800) pro tem. The dispute over ownership was meanwhile suspended.

In **2000** the situation changed when LDN by chance purchased the unrecognised James VI charter in Edinburgh, granting the barony to Murrays of Philiphaugh, fishing rights included. <u>This was a decisive moment.</u>

The Crown Estates therefore did not own Philiphaugh's rights in 1615. This re-opened the debate and gave the SAA powerful ammunition with which to argue its case. At last we had a foundation writ or charter.

In **2000/2** further researches and translations confirmed that the Crown has no title to fishings for Philiphaugh and doubtful ownership of Selkirk Burgh Water.

In **2003 (Oct)** Sheriff Kevin Drummond QC agreed to advise on the legal aspects of the case but only in a private capacity. Also, SAA and Philiphaugh Estates both agreed to press forward with a unified claim.

In **November 2003** enquiries were made to the Crown Estate stating that it was our belief that they were wrong in charging the SAA for the fishing rights that we in Selkirk believed were ours in the first place. In addition we now had evidence that they didn't own the fishings of Philiphaugh Estate either. It was felt that because he knew Ian Grant (Commissioner of the Crown Estate in Scotland) a claim would come better from a known figure than an unknown member of the Angling Association, so Sir David Steel (now Lord Steel of Aikwood from 1997) was enlisted and was willing to help. We had asked Sir David Steel to write to the CEC in a bid to find a remedy or resolution for our misgivings. He wrote outlining our case which basically stated the position from our standpoint.

On **10th November 2003** the letter from Sir David Steel was sent to Mr Grant declaring that the CEC should not be charging for something they didn't own. *(Appendix E)*

An important alliance concluded: Philiphaugh and Selkirk

As we pieced together the adverse claim, hoping thereby to convince the CEC of the merits of our case for Selkirk alone, we realised that our singular cause could greatly benefit from an alliance. Sir Michael Strang Steel, the present owner of Philiphaugh Estate, great grandson of William Strang Steel who had died in 1911, was willing to allow his Estate's claim of fishing rights on the Ettrick to be conjoined with the Burgh's rights in a single submission.

The Philiphaugh Estate also disputed the original HMW claims. Only much later did we discover and realise that the Haining Estate also had a small stretch of river bank for which they still owned the title to salmon fishing rights.

HMW had boldly stated that they owned all three fishing rights in their lease contract so we were misled. In fact they didn't own any fishing rights at all on the Ettrick! We discovered that, finally. *(See p. 31 & Ref 14)*

An adverse claim

On 13th Nov 2003 Ian Grant (IG) replied to Sir David Steel indicating he also desired a rapid resolution of the dispute. He stated that an adverse claim would need to be submitted to the Commission on the CE prescribed form and obligingly arranged for a copy to be sent. A copy of the adverse claim form is reproduced. *(Appendix F)*

Inter alia, Colin Cairney (chairman of SAA) wrote a letter to IG drafted by LDN and KD asking that the 2004 lease for the fishings, now due, be held in abeyance until the dispute is resolved.

Fiona Simpson, an administrator at the Scottish branch of CEC replied, repeating the demand for payment due for 2004. She said in her letter that if ownership was shown not to be the CEC's by March 31 2004, the rent would be repaid to the SAA. We also received a very terse reminder saying that the CEC would only consider our submission if we followed their standard adverse claims procedure. The form she sent came to the SAA along with detailed instructions on filling it in.

One of the pieces of advice on an adverse claim was that the CEC reserved a right to ask for "further information and evidence" which implied they could require evidence beyond foundation writs (their term for charters) and impose further research burdens on claimants. Initially they would consider a claim of ownership based only on these primary sources and the adverse claim would be judged on these alone. The demand for payment of the lease was becoming very insistent and we were given to understand that the undertaking to return the lease money was a major concession on their part.

The adverse claim process

The rules, what they consisted of and what we were permitted to submit

Our adverse claim, under CE rules, was hemmed in by restrictions. We had accumulated a thick file of supportive evidence but were not permitted to use much of it. We could only use "primary sources". This meant we needed original charters or certified copies, nothing else.

Prescriptive possession

In addition to the primary sources, we also had to show that we had prescriptive possession of the fishings of Philiphaugh Estate during the period preceding the Crown's claim of ownership of 1910-1914. We had to prove conclusively that people freely fished the Ettrick at Philiphaugh between 1890 when the Steels bought the estate and 1910, when HMW first declared their pursuit of ownership. In other words, show that salmon fishing was practiced freely by local people within the law and without interference from the Estate "openly, peaceably and without judicial interruption" when the Strang Steel family owned the estate. *(Appendices 11 & 12)*

We realised that proving Philiphaugh's ownership of their stretch would strengthen the case for Selkirk's portion, so we were casting around for such evidence. We were also aware it was going to be difficult to prove the so-called prescriptive possession part. At the time, all we had was vague recollections from Selkirk folk that their "grandfathers used to fish in the Ettrick" – but no hard evidence. Then the solution to this problem emerged.

William Strang Steel's affidavit

In the Philiphaugh Estate's private correspondence that we subsequently unearthed was a letter from HMW asking the Estate to describe the manner that the fishing had been done in the 40 years before 1910. William Strang Steel's lawyer had created an affidavit awaiting signature. *(Appendix 1)* The affidavit is lengthy and the quality too poor for reproduction. Instead a 1897 letter proving the prescriptive possession was found along with the Philiphaugh lawyer's understanding of the agreement. *(Appendix K)* In the event, William died before signing and it was his inheriting son Samuel who signed the affidavit, confirming that prescriptive possession had been fulfilled during the critical period. *(See page 28)* We were unaware of the existence of this deed at the time of our submission to the CEC, but it later proved that the necessary prescriptive possession part of ownership had actually already been achieved. The affidavit simply said that the Estate and various other people had fished there in the critical period without hindrance.

So we now had proof of the title and prescriptive possession for Philiphaugh. We needed the same for the Burgh of Selkirk.

The Adverse Claim to the Crown Estate

The extent of our submission, with a note about the loss of the Burgh records

When we started putting together the adverse claim to the Crown Estates our knowledge was limited: all we had to go on was the widespread local belief there had been free salmon fishing at one time for the Selkirk townsfolk where the Ettrick runs through the town. This fishing was reported practiced on the Town Water but extended upstream to Murray's Cauld. This was unsupported oral evidence and unacceptable to the CEC. So proving Selkirk's ownership was going to be a problem. We cast about for any references to fishing in all the archives we could think of. But we needed charters and proof of prescription.

There were oblique references to fishing in three charters from the 12th Century, only one of which remained extant. (The survivor was the charter of King Malcolm IV of 1159 in which he confirmed the grant of land and fishings to the monks of the original Selkirk Abbey and confirmed the abbey's removal to Kelso). *(Ref 1)*

The charter relevant to the actual granting of Burgh status to Selkirk (approx 1138 AD) and the earlier abbey charters were lost, probably when the Burgh was sacked in 1418.* However, there was the more recent re-granted charter to the Burgh in the 16th century. *(Ref 13)* This last charter, still in existence, simply confirmed Burgh rights but had made no particular mention of fishing. We could however supply photocopies of the earlier charter of 1159 and the one from 1536.

After a great deal of digging and finding our way into many cul-de-sacs we finally completed

---

*Selkirk got sacked in 1418 – and how it lost its ancient Charters

Along with other Border towns, Selkirk was sacked in 1418 by a force led by Sir Robert d'Umfraville, an Agincourt veteran and Governor of Berwick by then in English hands.

This was in retaliation and revenge for raids into England by Scots and was part of the general unrest of the period. It was the time when The Scots King, James I, was a prisoner in England in the hands of King Henry V. All Selkirk's ancient documents were presumably burned at that time.

our list of items to be lodged with the Crown Estates in our dispute of ownership. Here is our inventory:

Adverse claim dossier, submitted on 11th March 2004:*

1. Charter, March 1536 from King James V, re-granting burgh status to Selkirk.

2. Charter, 1159 from King Malcolm IV, confirming grants to monks of Selkirk Abbey and also rights to fish to "My People" of Selkirk.

3. Acta Parliamentorum Carolus II, (Charles II) 1681, giving away most of Selkirk Commonty.

4. Disposition by Sir John FPN Murray, 1889, selling Philiphaugh Estate with details.

5. Selkirk Burgh Council Minutes, details from 1910-1914, copies of relevant entries.

6. Tourist's Guide and Angler's Companion 1893; salmon fishing in the Ettrick – details.
    (Ref 6)

7. Charter, 1615 from King James VI elevating Philiphaugh to a new barony.

8. Acta Parliamentorum Gulielmi III, 1702, confirming 1615 charter.

9. Particulars of sale of Philiphaugh Estate, 1888, which included salmon fishing rights.
    (Ref 11 & 12)

---

*All of these items of paperwork were submitted either in their entirety, as certified extracts or as certified photocopies and translations from the Latin where necessary. A brief description of their relevance to the case was included: but no other documents were included as the restrictive adverse claims format dictated. These were the documents in support of our adverse claim. We realised our claim for Selkirk was weak (Ref 15) but we had more confidence in our case for Philiphaugh.

The proof of ownership for the Philiphaugh fishings was much more secure since we now had the original charter of 1615 from King James I or VI granting the fishing rights as part of the barony. We had not yet discovered the existence of the affidavit of Samuel Strang Steel delivered to HMW in 1912 confirming the prescriptive possession of the fishings by Philiphaugh Estate. We did discover it later as mentioned above. We also unearthed a letter giving a Mr Brown permission to fish in 1897, further proof of Philiphaugh's prescriptive possession. (Appendix K)

We are against an imperious adversary: what do we hope to achieve, and how?

The diary of events which follows dates from March 2004 when we submitted our claim to the CEC. It records the difficult and tortuous process of combating a powerful and over bearing national body who were giving no quarter. We have to admit nevertheless, and give them their due, that the CEC were unfailingly and studiously polite throughout their entire correspondence with us.

We hoped that success and the return of the fishing rights might be achieved by persistence, painstaking research and dogged resistance to any form of legalised bullying. We also hoped that others might learn from our experiences and manage to recover community property which may or may not have been appropriated by powerful organisations in the past by nefarious means. Our journey has therefore been charted in detail.

We believed that the ownership of only two fishing rights were worth disputing, those belonging to Philiphaugh Estate and also Selkirk Burgh's. The rights of the Haining Estate was deemed a lost cause. We wrongly assumed that the CEC had legally taken possession of those rights. They told us that the Haining rights were theirs and we believed them. Sir Robert Clerk again made the assertion of the Crown's ownership in January 2006. This statement was made in front of witnesses and was a re-statement of the Crown's claim in 1912. *(Ref 5)* As it turned out, we should have known better and we were naïve to have taken them at their word.

As far as the title to the Selkirk stretch was concerned, we had only the original charter from 1159 granting the fishing to the monks of Selkirk Abbey. We also had several charters bestowing the rights to fish along with the barony of Selkirk granted to the Douglases. But as these barony rights were rescinded by an act of 1747, we thought that they were irrelevant to our argument.

[Later we realised in an 'esprit d'escalier' that Selkirk Burgh in fact had inherited the Douglas rights including the fishings following the 1747 Act and the records were indeed relevant to our cause. The Douglas Baron of Selkirk was compensated by the government, (inadequately in his opinion), for his loss of authority in 1747, as were many others likewise. *(Appendix D)*

We had faithfully transcribed records of letters from HMW to Selkirk Burgh Council and recorded in Council minutes from 1910-1914, but we believed that none of the original letters to the Council had survived. *(Appendix C)*

Events of 2004

Over and above the permissible list we had many other references and documentary confirmations of Selkirk's involvement in the fishing supporting our case. However, because they were not foundation writs, they were classed as inadmissible under the Crown Estates rules and were consequently not submitted as part of the evidence. Although they could not be sent in they certainly supported and confirmed our claim so we were hopeful they might be admissible at a later date.

Mar 11th - The adverse claim submitted on behalf of Selkirk and Philiphaugh was duly acknowledged by the CEC.

March 31st - The deadline unilaterally fixed by Fiona Simpson of the CEC passed. Ownership had not been resolved so the CEC ruled that the 2004 lease money, already demanded and paid, was not repayable. The SAA had paid this leasing charge for 2004 during 2003 but hoped to recover it. The time it would take for the CEC to process the complex paperwork really precluded any reimbursement for the 2004 lease within the three weeks remaining. So we accepted this.

August 24th - Because the SAA had heard nothing from the CEC since submitting the adverse claim in March and despite writing frequently, at our instigation Sir David Steel again wrote to Ian Grant (IG) of the CEC asking what progress was being made.

August 25th - A letter from Anderson Strathern (CEC's lawyers) was received asking for more details of the delineation of the stretches claimed. We remained unaware that the Haining Estate still held rights on the river.

September 3rd - LDN supplied the details following their request and submitted to Anderson Strathern a coloured map of the extent of the beats involved.

September 6th - Sir DS received a response to his enquiry as to progress from IG claiming our case was still being dealt with promptly. IG gave an assurance that the lease was still active until 2007 despite the dispute. This was an implied threat as the annual lease had been paid at the due date but we were being subtly reminded that the lease could be re-arranged with someone else if Selkirk proved difficult. At least that was how we read the letter.

September 28th - Further maps, interpretation and documents were supplied by LDN with advice and input from KD. Basically we had received a further request for a breakdown in the proportions of the river that could be apportioned to each estate. This was done and receipt acknowledged.

Six months had now passed, but we were happy to supply the additional information requested.

A summary of the submission to CEC on behalf of Selkirk Angling Association and Philiphaugh Estate, Selkirk.

In answer to a second request for more detail on 24th August 2004 and sent to CEC on the 3rd September.

We based our claim on the following and responded comprehensively:

Charters

1. The foundation writ on which we rely is the surviving Charter of King Malcolm IV of 1159 which is a grant 'ad piscandum'.

The original grant was in Earl David's Charter of 1119 and in the Charter of 1147 by Earl David when he became King David. Neither of these charters survived, but both are transcribed into the Liber Santa Maria de Calchou. the Kelso Book from Kelso Abbey, written circa 1330. They were transcriptions, translations and commentary and were all framed in like terms with regard to the fishings. King Malcolm IV confirmed the earlier charters. *(Ref 1)*

The James V Charter of 1535 explains some of the difficulties viz. "whereas the charters…of the Burgh of Selkirk…have for the most part been destroyed through assaults of war." It is fortunate that this and the 1159 Charters both survive. *(Ref 13)*

We discovered in 2006 – long after we had submitted our adverse claim – much more evidence of the town's ownership and custody of the fishings. This was a welcome discovery but would not have been admissible evidence even if we had found it earlier. The CEC's imposed restrictions would have disqualified it. Because the CEC had requested more information, we were able to include previously excluded material.

2. The destruction, referred to by King James V, of many of the original documents linked to the Common lands of Selkirk undoubtedly contributed to the constant disputes which resulted finally in the Great Arbitration of 1678. This was confirmed by, and became, the Act of Charles II of 1681. *(Ref 23)*

The Act of 1681 - Selkirk was bullied into surrendering 88% of its common land. An attempt was being made, after much disputation over many years, to settle the differences between the Burgh and the surrounding landowners.

We said this to the CEC (really throwing sand in their lawyers' eyes!):

"This document can make for turgid reading with its repeated reference to local geography and topography; but closer analysis can prove to be instructive. The preamble to the Act tells us where we are going. It is an Act to ratify the decree arbitral "for the division of the Commonty of Selkirk." It contains detailed bounding descriptions of all the disputed lands. For our present purposes it fixes the boundaries of all proprietors on the Ettrick and I have prepared a fresh plan showing those boundaries in accordance with the Act.

That part of the southern side of the Ettrick bordering on the Burgh itself is not specifically included in the arbitration as it was not disputed. It is covered in general terms in the act by the passage "It is always hereby declared" (421 L col.). *(See map p.4)*

For your assistance I now describe in summary the content of the Act of 1681:

1. It begins by describing the parties and sets out the terms of the submission to arbitration. Notably the parties include William Kerr of Sunderlandhall, other landowners or their representatives and two named Baillies of the Burgh of Selkirk "on behalf of the Counsellors and Comontie of the said Burgh."

    It records that "the great and vast bounds of ground called the Comon of Selkirk… hes for these many ages past…been the seed and ground of much trouble contention and debate amongst them for which they are most solicitous for the future to remead." To bring the matter to a satisfactory conclusion the issue was remitted to the named arbiters for the purpose of determining what parts of the Common lands of Selkirk shall belong in all time coming to each of the parties to the arbitration, and for excluding and debarring all other pretenders from troubling them in the peaceful possession of their portions of the Common.

2. The whole parties bound and obliged themselves and their heirs to stand and abide by and fulfil the terms of the decree arbitral and consented to registration thereof in the Books of Council and Session. The whole parties then subscribed.

3. It then continues that the arbiters appointed, having on several days and diets met upon the ground of the Commonty of Selkirk, having perambulated the marches and "having taken exact information anent their interests and possessions…and considering the dangerous consequences of the manyfold actions and pleyes (quarrels) that hes occurred amongst the saids pairties tending severall times to the disturbance of the peace and the great expence and trouble of the pairties", determine and divide "from Comontie to propertie" the lands after specified "in all time comeing" as they have meithed (marked), marched, designated and divided.

4 "To witt, in the South Common of the Burgh of Selkirk we have divided from Comontie to propertie and decernes the same to pertain in heretage to the said Burgh of Selkirk *that part of the said common which begins at the east side of Selkirk Loaning…and then goes eastward by the Kingcroft dyke…by the south side of the Potloch*" (my italics). The description then continues for the next column and a half to identify in precise detail the part of the Common that is divided from the Commonty and becomes a "propertie" in favour of the Burgh of Selkirk and its inhabitants.

5. There then follow a number of "Items" which are of no relevance to this submission beyond that each is a division of property from Commonty to property, in the named proprietors, from the Commonty of Selkirk.

6. At 424 "**Item** as to that pairt of the foresaid Comontie Comonlie called the North Common we Descerne to pertain in property *to the said Burgh of Selkirk and inhabitants thereof* which wee…separat from the Comontie in maner foresaid *That pairt and portion of…the said North Comon Begining at the merch stone upon the north syd of the water of Ettrick just opposite to the Cobleheugh…and then goes eastward down the water of Ettrick till it comes to the Nettlieburn*

foot, and then goes up the said burn while it comes to the Linglie moss" thence *northward etc.* (my italics) the description then advancing until it returns to the Philipburn.

7. The next "Item", not surprisingly in terms of the geography being followed, is JM of Philiphaugh where there is divided from the Commonty ***"begining at the foot of Philipburn and goes down the north syd of the water of Ettrick"*** (there again follows a detailed bounding description back round to the Philipburn), ***"reserveing always to the said Burgh of Selkirk and Inhabitants thereof free ishe and entrie…for transporting of turffs"*** but excluding pasturage ***"declareing also that if the water of Ettrick shall alter the present current thereof whereby the Milnes Calds and Dams of Selkirk may be prejudged through want of water. In that case it shall be laufull to the said burgh to make a new Cald and cast ane new Dame in any place most convenient for bringing the water to their milnes giveing them hereby plenam potestam aqueductus in the case foresaid"*** (my italics).

8   The next three "Items" are not relevant to this submission.

9. The items at 426 L re. Wm. Kerr of Sunderlandhall, Thomas Kerr of Ovenscloss and JE of Bridgeheugh provide the descriptions of the boundaries which we have shown on our new map.

10. The arbiters then "Decerne and Ordain" the foregoing divisions from the Commonty of Selkirk to the submitters in all time coming, make an order for expenses, fix a penalty of £500 Scots for failure to observe the decree arbitral and the deed is then subscribed.

Thereafter His Majesty, with the advice and consents of the Estates of Parliament, ratifies the decree to stand in all time coming and dispenses with **"all imperfections and objections that may be proponed against it"** for ever.

Commentary on the foregoing Act

The Act of 1681 is an important document for a number of reasons which I now enumerate:

1. The document records the extent of the Selkirk Common being great and vast bounds which have been a source of problems for generations past.

2. It deals with an area of land that considerably exceeds the area with which we are now concerned, e.g. it deals also with Yair and Fairnilee which abound the Tweed.

3. The allocations from the Commonty cover the whole extent of the River Ettrick so far as it is relevant to the present claim on behalf of the Selkirk Angling Association and Philiphaugh Estates.

4. It includes the whole of the Ettrick from the Meeting of the Waters (where Yarrow branches off) to its meeting with the river Tweed.

5. All of the riparian proprietors have their land boundaries determined by grants from the Commonty of Selkirk. This is, it must be borne in mind, neither a grant of lands nor a disposition. It is a determination of boundary disputes between heritable proprietors.

6. In particular the marches between Selkirk Commonty, Ovenscloss and Sunderlandhall can be identified without difficulty and are marked on the map attached.

Philiphaugh

7. The right of Salmon Fishing presently asserted by the Crown includes that part of the River Ettrick belonging to Philiphaugh Estate.

8. Philiphaugh is a Barony title granted by King James VI in 1615. Therefore, to the extent that the right to Salmon Fishing is asserted over Philiphaugh,

that claim is unfounded. Philiphaugh Estate was sold with Salmon Fishings in 1888. Selkirk Angling Club, and prior to them Selkirk Burgh Council, have been paying rent since 1912 to the Crown Estates and its predecessors in respect of some 60% of the length of the leased waters of the Ettrick which actually belong to Philiphaugh.

Selkirk Commonty

9. To the extent that the Submission to Arbitration related to the subdivision of parts of Selkirk Commonty only where there had been boundary disputes, those parts of the Commonty not referred to remain part of Selkirk Common. Therefore the area highlighted dotted pink on the plan remains part of Selkirk Commonty.

Conclusions

1. Selkirk Commonty holds a grant ad piscandum by Royal Charter.

2. Selkirk Commonty includes by reference to the Act of 1681 that part of the Ettrick over which the Crown Estate Commissioners have asserted rights.

3. Philiphaugh Estate is a Barony title including rights to Salmon Fishing and part of whose boundaries include a further part of the River Ettrick over which the Crown Estate Commissioners have asserted rights.

Signed, Dr. L.D.Neil 21/9/2004

Additional Evidence

Additional supportive evidence

We discovered in 2006 – long after we had submitted our adverse claim – much more evidence of the town's ownership and custody of the fishings. This was a welcome discovery but would not have been admissible evidence even if we had found it earlier. The CEC's imposed restrictions would have disqualified it. *(Appendix G & p 70)*

The important new discoveries were:

a) Extract from Burgh Court Book of Selkirk

15 January 1537/38. Court held by alderman and bailies. 'Inquest'* of 14.

> "And attour this inquest dischairgis maister Thomas Ker, procuratour for Rynyan Smyth, in time cummyng to set nettis within fredome and heritaigis of Selkyrk and specially in the vatter of the sammyn…"

> [And over and above, this inquest forbids Mister Thomas Ker, lawyer for Rynyan Smyth, in time coming to place nets within the boundaries of Selkirk and especially in the water of the same."] *(Ref 40)*

Comment

The significance of this archival record is that the official body of the Burgh is administering the fishings in what is clearly the Burgh Waters. This was two years after the 1535 charter of James V re-granting Burgh rights. The 1535 charter therefore in affirming Burgh rights, inter alia, affirmed the title to the fishings as being a Burgh right proven by this court record (supplied by local historian Walter Elliot).

---

*An inquest was a 'judicial and administrative body in Burghs'.

b) **Council Minutes**

By checking Burgh Council minutes during the 19th Century, we discovered that the Council had let out the fishings to various individuals, for example in 1802, 1818, 1820 and 1826.

This confirmed that the Council had prescriptive possession in the period before the Angling Club was inaugurated (1866) and the Burgh's right of ownership allowing the Council to let out the Burgh property.

c) **Judicial notices** warning of illegal fishing and ensuing penalties from 1806 & 1817. *(pps 167/168) (Appendix B)*

d) **A Council minute** appealing for help from Selkirk citizens to help repair the town cauld. An extract from the Selkirk Court book and Burgh Council minute from 1713 details that the Burgh had responsibility and ownership of the cauld which had become damaged. This was further evidence of ownership. Under the old Scots Law dictum "In aedificatum solo, solo cedit", "What is built on the land, belongs to it." *(Ref 16)*

e) **Burgh Rights**

Normally burghs had control of their fishings. Quotes from:
Mercat Cross and Tolbooth by Craig Mair, 1988 (Publisher, John Donald) *(Ref 3)*

f) **Rental of Burgh Fishings**

Valuation Rolls submitted to the Royal 'Burrows' Convention, 1714, details demands for rental returns for fishings in the Burgh of Selkirk. *(Ref 2)*

g) **Burgh privileges**

PhD Thesis from GS Pryde, St Andrews Univ. 1926. *(Ref 3)*

The reason for submitting such a detailed reply to the CEC was intentionally so that their lawyers would have to involve themselves in substantial reading and checking while clocking up costly lawyer hours for the CEC. It also enabled us to add evidence in addition to that which their adverse claim format demanded. They asked for detail, we gave it to them.

The Rejection

Dec. 7th 2004. Anderson Strathern wrote, nine months after the submission, to reject both claims, that of Selkirk Burgh and also that of Philiphaugh Estate. *(See Appendix H)*

The manner of rejection

Our payment for the 2004 lease was made in November 2003 and the CE set a deadline of March 31st 2004 as the "refund" date to us if we were able to prove they did not own the fishing rights. As our adverse claim submission in the format demanded by them was not lodged until March 3rd 2004, the deadline was soon passed. On account of the volume of legal work involved, we could not complain. So the 2004 lease money, £4,700.00, went to the CEC.

Although we submitted our adverse claim in the correct format in March 2004, the CEC twice requested more information in September 2004. This was supplied. Six months after the initial submission a letter from Sir David Steel asking about progress had provoked a reply that the CE would address the matter "promptly". It turned out to be anything but prompt. The rejection was 9 months after submission.

It looked to us that the CEC was using delay as a tactic.

Note: *a) the adverse claim format specifically excluded such evidence as they now based their rejection on.*

b) nine months had elapsed before the CE rejected the SAA's legal right to claim, after they had insisted that they wanted the matter cleared up "promptly". (The OED does not support their interpretation of the meaning of 'promptness'!)

We now had to challenge what amounted to a totally unjustifiable rejection of our claim by the Crown received just in time for Christmas. This is what we said.

2005: SAA reply to the CEC's rejection

We collated our comments on the CEC rejection and submitted our reply to Anderson Strathern, the CEC's lawyer, on the 1st February 2005.

We said:

> "I refer to your letter dated 7 December in which you intimate the rejection of the claims to Salmon Fishings on the River Ettrick.
>
> I note the reasons given for the rejection and formally indicate that these reasons are not accepted as being well founded.
>
> I now deal with each of the reasons in turn:
>
> 1. **Philiphaugh Estate**: it is said that there has been exclusive possession of the salmon fishing rights by the Crown Estate since at least the end of the First World War and that no evidence of exclusive possession by the owners of Philiphaugh Estate has been presented.
>
>   It is, however, accepted that there appears to be a *habile* title. That was the only matter which we were in fact addressing in our submission and it is significant that that concession is now made.
>
>   My reason for adopting the course of addressing only the status of the title was that it had not been accepted by your predecessors in title in 1912 that there <u>was</u> a habile title when this disputed issue was left to proceed on an "experimental" basis. (Ownership was indeed accepted in a different letter of which we have a copy.)
>
>   Before embarking on any exploration of the consequences which flow from the recognition of Philiphaugh's *habile* title, the following is, in my respectful opinion, determinative of the issue between us so far as the Philiphaugh

water is concerned: the determination of the boundaries for Philiphaugh can be taken for convenience as being fixed by the Act of 1681. From that date Philiphaugh Estate possessed the fishing rights continuously, openly and peaceably without judicial interruption until 1889 when the salmon fishing rights were sold _nominatim_ with the Estate.

That single period of possession was plainly in itself sufficient to complete the title to the salmon fishings in the proprietor of Philiphaugh. **(LA vs MCCulloch, 1875, 2R 27.)**

In addition, the fact of possession as is now asserted by you is not accepted. The present proprietor of Philiphaugh has fished part of the Philiphaugh waters continuously and continues to do so to the present day. It is clear that the right now asserted by you relates to only part of the whole of Philiphaugh fishings and, as you will be well aware, there is ample authority that it is unnecessary for the proprietor of Philiphaugh to have fished every individual pool or stretch of the water in order to defeat your claim to part thereof. _(See map p.23)_
(Lord Advocate v Lovat 1880 7R (HL) 122)

You have seen the particulars of sale of Philiphaugh in 1889 including salmon fishings which we submitted to you and we will, if it is considered necessary, provide statements confirming the exercise of the right of fishings over the remainder of the Philiphaugh water.

I turn now to the right of Selkirk Angling Association to assert the claim

2   **Selkirk Angling Association:** Your first assertion is that SAA has no right to submit this claim: once again this is simply an aspect of the claim which I had not found it necessary to expand upon.

With regard to the right to submit the claim, Scottish Borders Council is of course the statutory successor to Selkirk Burgh Council for its statutory undertakings. Selkirk and District Angling Association (to give the Association its full formal designation) has existed since before 1882 and was formally appointed by Selkirk Burgh Council to manage and maintain the fishings on behalf of the Burgh in 1967. It continues to do so. The Association has, on that authority, issued the permits since that time and, as you are aware, pays the rent.

You should also be aware that the heritable proprietor of the remaining substantial Selkirk commonty (which includes the riparian land adjoining the disputed fishings) is the Selkirk Common Good Fund, which, for purely administrative reasons of convenience is conducted through Scottish Borders Council.

The Selkirk Common Good Fund also holds, on behalf of the community of Selkirk, farms, lands and other buildings which continue to be administered for the exclusive benefit of the population of Selkirk. It is our contention that the relevant salmon fishing rights are vested in the riparian proprietor, namely Selkirk Common Good Fund.

We will provide authority from the Selkirk Common Good Fund and SBC confirming their approval and our right to maintain this claim if so required.

A substantive issue in relation to the Charter of 1535/6 by James V is raised and I will return to this, but before doing so I address the question of the assertion again made that CEC has had exclusive possession since at least the end of the First World War.

That is an assertion which is wholeheartedly refuted.

The correspondence between the Burgh Clerk and HM Woods in 1912 establishes beyond any doubt that the arrangement then entered into between the Burgh Council and HM Woods was one which was temporary and contentious. It was an arrangement which was entered into on behalf of the Council, as the Council Minutes disclose, purely to retain the fishings for the benefit of the public "until such time as the Crown has completed their investigation of the titles".

With regard to your observations on the Charter of 1535/36 by James V which you describe as granted "of new", you understandably proceed on the basis that that is the foundation charter and that the absence of any reference to fishings does not found a *habile* title.

That of course finds its source in our summary which accompanied our further submissions of 28th Sept which referred to the fact that it is fortunate that the 1535 and 1159 Charters both survive. Our first submission (of which the above was only a summary) referred at p.2 to the content of the earlier Charters.

I am sorry if I did not make our position crystal clear but will now do so.

The approach which you have adopted of treating the Charter of 1535/6 as the starting point is perhaps understandable given the tortuous history of the Selkirk Charters but is mistaken. I can do no better than quote King James himself when he says in the Charter of 1535/6 that

> ...." *Whereas the charters* (note plural) *of the old foundation of the Burgh of Selkirk .... have for the most part* (note "most") *been destroyed through assaults of war etc... the king has of new infeft to the burgesses and community (of) Selkirk etc..."*

What that Charter does not do is repeal or discharge any earlier charter but simply recognises that some of the charters have been destroyed. The Charter of 1159 of Malcolm IV survives and contains the grant "...et aquas meas circa Selcherche communes ad piscandum suis p'p'lis ut meis..."

This is our grant. For the avoidance of doubt I also pray in aid as further support the Charters of 1119 and 1147.

From 1912 the situation regarding the Selkirk Water proceeded on an experimental basis "until the question of title is resolved". As with so much of Selkirk's history, wars once again intervened, in this case two World Wars, and no further work was done to resolve the issue of title.

We now say that experiment is at an end and the title dispute is resolved in our favour. The prescriptive possession upon which you found has throughout that time been a challenged right as is clearly evidenced from the records which exist and cannot be relied upon to found open and peaceable prescriptive possession.

In addition, as I have pointed out above, approximately one half of the Water in respect of which we have been paying rent is in fact Water belonging to Philiphaugh Estates. Furthermore, there exists an affidavit testifying to the unopposed fishing of the water since the Strang Steel purchase.

In summary, therefore, it is now asserted that you have no right to the Philiphaugh Water and Selkirk Common Good Fund has a stateable claim to the Selkirk Water which, on its own and without the Philiphaugh Water can only be of a nominal value at best.

It would be unfortunate if this matter required to be judicially determined in the public domain at the present time and we trust that on considering this matter further it will be able to be decorously resolved between us."

Signed SAA

Our own assessment then

Philiphaugh's claim was rejected in the CEC's letter although it had admitted grudgingly that "it appears" Philiphaugh had a habile title but because it had not been shown that they had "exclusive possession" of their fishing rights prior to the CEC claim. The CEC claimed to have had exclusive possession since "at least the end of the First World War", and therefore Philiphaugh could not now claim to own the fishing rights. We were stunned by this assertion by one of the leading legal firms in the country. Acting on behalf of the Crown, they had ignored their predecessor's undertakings, ignored the law on fishing and manipulated the facts to suit their case.

Selkirk Burgh's claim through the SAA was further rejected on the grounds that there was no direct link between the Scottish Borders Council (directed by statute under the 1973 Local Government (Scotland) Act and the 1995 Act to administer the Common Good) with Selkirk Burgh Council. Therefore, they concluded, Selkirk Angling Association had no right or legal standing to be submitting an adverse claim on behalf of Selkirk's Common Good. They demanded that the council gives evidence that the Angling Association had their approval to be lodging an adverse claim.

The rejection letter was also keen to point out that there was no direct grant of fishings in the 1535/36 charter. The burgh therefore, they concluded, had no habile title. We had to admit to ourselves that Selkirk's claim was based on less solid ground than Philiphaugh's. We did not have a charter specifying the Burgh's fishing rights and the various communications in the Council minutes, although extensive, were transcriptions, with no original documents.

This was about to change dramatically!

Our immediate task was to confirm the position of the SAA as the negotiator on behalf of the Burgh. Scottish Borders Council raised several objections and hesitated to endorse the role of the SAA.

A letter from Sir David Steel was sent to the Crown Estate ridiculing the agency's apparent ignorance of the sequence of administrative responsibility from Burgh Council to Scottish Borders Council.

A reply from the Crown Estate clarifying their approach and blaming a "typographical error" for the assumption that the SAA had "no right" to represent Selkirk, was received within three days. In actual fact it was the obtuseness of the legal department of Scottish Borders Council that had tried to obstruct our progress.

There was also acknowledgement of receipt of the lease for the 2005 fishing season amounting to £4,700 which was paid in **December 2004**. This was paid under protest and an assurance obtained that if the fishing rights were proven not to be the Crown's property by **31st December, 2005**, the leasing charge would be returned. **These dates proved to be significant.**

Some other important dates in 2005

Jan 17th: Letter from Fiona Simpson (of CEC) acknowledging 2005 payment of the 2006 lease and undertaking to refund rent if the dispute **is resolved by 31st Dec. 2005.**

Jan & Feb: Prolonged correspondence with SBC lawyers Anne Isles and Ian Wilkie who unhelpfully and persistently questioned the right of the SAA to be making representations on behalf of the Selkirk Common Good. The matter was resolved by the letter from Sir David Steel to the CEC of 24th Jan. expressing astonishment at the Crown's assertions.

Feb 3rd: Apologetic email from Fiona Simpson of CEC to LDN blaming a typographical error for implying that SAA had no right to be making a claim. Sir DS receives a similar letter 8/2/06 from IG. This was a gracious admission but we recognised that the real omission/fault lay with the legal department of SBC.

The climate then suddenly changed!

The Glasgow miracle

Amazing discovery II, February 10th, 2005

During the prolonged negotiations with the Crown Estate, we had kept Glasgow solicitor Graham Philips of Morisons WS in Glasgow, who acted for the Philiphaugh Estate and the Strang Steel family, fully informed of any developments. His input and advice had proved very valuable on many occasions. We found out that there are several branches of the Strang Steel family in various places in Scotland and some used the same legal firm.

One branch of the family in another part of Scotland used a lawyer who was also a partner alongside Graham Philips in the same Glasgow law firm.

This lawyer had been walking along a corridor one day in their office in Glasgow. In the corridor was a pile of deed boxes that had been temporarily stacked there while the cellar containing boxes of old documents was being repainted.

On top of the pile was a box marked 'Strang Steel'. This deed box was just on the point of being returned to the dark cellar where it had come from along with the other deed boxes, probably to be forgotten for several more decades.

Intrigued, he opened the box to discover on the top a large file labelled 'Salmon Fishing, Philiphaugh'. Aware that his partner Graham Philips had been dealing with fishings belonging to the Philiphaugh branch of the family, he had a quick look at the contents. Realising there could be some important and relevant correspondence on fishings he photocopied all these original letters and handed the copies to Graham Philips. He in turn forwarded the newly discovered material to Sir Michael Strang Steel as well as to the SAA.

These letters and documents, preserved and re-discovered by pure chance, would normally have been destroyed many years ago but somehow had survived simply by being forgotten in a lawyer's cellar.

The correspondence turned out to be original copies of letters and represented virtually all the correspondence between HMW and Philiphaugh Estate on the fishings from 1910 to 1925.

The letters confirmed that the Estate had never relinquished their rights to the fishings and the Crown therefore had no right to claim them. The file also corroborated the synopsis of correspondence which the Selkirk Burgh Council clerk had faithfully copied into the Burgh Minutes between 1910 and 1914.

In particular, the letters confirmed:

a) That the lease charges for the fishings agreed by HMW were to be nominal.

b) That any arrangement agreed would be "experimental". *(Appendix K)*

c) That the arrangements were only "temporary". *(Appendix M)*

d) That the declared ownership of Philiphaugh rights by HMW was disputed by Philiphaugh right up until the lease agreement was signed.

e) That HMW undertook to investigate the true ownership of the rights (but we know now that they never did).

f) That Philiphaugh was subsequently acknowledged by HMW in 1912 as the true owner of the rights to the fishings that they had earlier claimed.

g) The documents also contained a copy of the affidavit attesting to the use of the fishing rights during the 19th century which had been drawn up for William Strang Steel and after his death signed by his son Samuel.

All of this was irrefutable evidence that HMW had not only been riding roughshod over the ownership rights of the Philiphaugh Estate, but also laid out the (bogus) assurances given to the parties involved to cajole them to accede to the Crown's wishes. To their great credit it also confirmed the veracity of the Burgh Council minutes' transcriptions. *(Appendix C)*

CEC claim the Haining Water

Our researches were complete: we had uncovered enough to refute the Crown's claims and counter their objections to granting our adverse claim.

However, we were also now verbally made aware that the CEC considered they owned the rights to the Haining stretch of water.

Among the Philiphaugh papers in the Glasgow hoard was a copy of the letter from 1912, in which Mr Norman Seth Pringle-Pattison, owner of the Haining Estate, relinquished, through his lawyer, "any claim" on the Haining fishing rights. *(Appendix N.)* We had decided to keep this information and the copy of the letter to ourselves in case the CEC was unaware of its existence! The CEC soon put us right!

The meeting at Philiphaugh 13/4/05

Feb 16th: Letter sent to AS by LDN (composed largely by KD) asserting the Crown Estates were legally wholly in error in their rejection of Selkirk's and Philiphaugh's claims, both on the basis of the previous evidence and also as a result of the new evidence found in Glasgow. We were now far better armed!

We suggested a meeting to discuss our evidence and to invite their views on the recently discovered correspondence. *(Appendix U.)*

Mar. 1st: A letter was received from AS addressed to LDN accepting a meeting in principle.

The venue suggested was at the Anderson Strathern offices in Edinburgh. We were not at all keen to meet there and suggested a local venue.

After a little delay, a meeting was arranged to be held at Philiphaugh House on 13th April following our refusal to meet in Edinburgh.

We produced and circulated a proposed agenda and a list of additional documents prior to the meeting.

This was going to be a crucially important meeting between representatives of Anderson Strathern (Crown Estates), Scottish Borders Council, Selkirk and District Angling Association and Philiphaugh Estates. In the event, the local authority representatives failed to turn up.

Meeting to review the ownership of salmon fishing rights on the river Ettrick currently leased to Selkirk Angling Association by Crown Estates.

Draft Agenda

To be held at 11 am, 13th April 2005, Philiphaugh, Selkirk.

1. **Sederunt** and introductions.

2. **Apologies:** Sir David Steel, Mr Ian Wilkie, Anne Isles.

3. Brief summary of events leading to the present. (Dr Neil)

4. Consideration of claims to ownership of salmon fishing rights:
    a) The Philiphaugh Estate stretch.
    b) The Selkirk Burgh stretch.

The relevant documents have already been provided.

5. Proposals for resolution of the dispute.

Lunch is kindly provided by Lady Strang Steel. The meeting will continue afterwards if necessary.

Dr. Lindsay Neil. 4/4/5.

Sir Michael Strang Steel

Mr Ian Wilkie, SBC

Mr David Mitchell, SAA

Mr Graham M Philips of Morisons WS

Diana Thurston-Smith, Anderson Strathern

Alisdair Wilson from SAA

Anne Isles, SBC

Councillor V. Davidson, SBC

Sheriff Kevin Drummond QC

Lord Steel of Aikwood

Jim Drysdale, Anderson Strathern

Jackie Wilson, from SBC will take minutes

Documents relevant to the meeting on 13th April, 2005, and some already provided:

Relating to Philiphaugh:

1. Original barony charter of 1615, (already provided)

2. Charter confirmation in Parliament 1701 (already provided)

3. Correspondence between HMW, Philiphaugh Estates and various legal firms, 1910 – 1925

4. Synopsis of lease HMW to Selkirk Town Council dated 6 Oct 1914 *(Ref 14)*

5. Letter from William Strang Steel to Mr Brown, 1897 *(Appendix K)*

Relating to Haining Estate:

Letter from Curle, Melrose Feb 1912 *(Appendix N)*

Relating to Selkirk Burgh:

1. Charter of removal from Malcolm IV, 1159 (already provided)

2. Act detailing Lordship and barony of Selkirk granted to Archibald, Lord Douglas by Mary Queen of Scots 1567 'Cum piscariis' *(see Appendix D under 1567)*

3. Charter giving to William, Lord Douglas the free 'Burgh of Barony' of Selkirk, amongst others, by James VI. 1602 'Cum piscariis'. *(Appendix D)*

4. Act of George II of 1747 (C43) abolishing Stewartries, Regalities etc. and Burghs of Barony (confirmed in the 1795 Act re-establishing some) *(Appendix D)*

5. Two public notices issued by the Procurator Fiscal of Selkirk of 1806 and 1817 confirming legal jurisdiction over fishing in the Ettrick *(Appendix B)*

6. Extract of Town Council minutes showing the town's responsibility for the upkeep of the cauld in the Ettrick at Selkirk *(Ref 16)*

Minutes of the meeting were produced thanks to Scottish Borders Council who were a disinterested (i.e. unbiased) body with regard to the fishing dispute. The minutes are reproduced here in their entirety as taken by Jackie Wilson.

....

SALMON FISHING RIGHTS - SELKIRK

MINUTE of MEETING between REPRESENTATIVES OF MESSRS ANDERSON STRATHERN, SCOTTISH BORDERS COUNCIL, SELKIRK AND DISTRICT ANGLING ASSOCIATION and PHILIPHAUGH ESTATES held at PHILIPHAUGH, SELKIRK on WEDNESDAY, 13 APRIL 2005 at 11.00am.

Present: Diana Thurston-Smith and Mr Jim Drysdale, Anderson Strathern (on behalf of the Crown Estates)

Sir Michael Strang Steel and Mr Graham Philips, Morisons, WS (Philiphaugh Estates)

Councillor Vicky Davidson (Scottish Borders Council)

Mr David Mitchell and Mr Alastair Wilson (Selkirk Angling Association)

Sheriff Kevin Drummond, QC

Dr. Lindsay Neil

Apologies: Sir David Steel

               Ian Wilkie and Anne Isles - Scottish Borders Council

In attendance: Administrative Officer, Corporate Resources, Scottish Borders Council
               (Mrs J. Wilson)

WELCOME AND INTRODUCTIONS

1. Sir Michael Strang Steel opened the meeting by welcoming those present and extending his appreciation to all for attending, in particular the representatives of Anderson Strathern on behalf of the Crown Estates.

BRIEF SUMMARY OF EVENTS LEADING TO PRESENT

2. Dr Lindsay Neil provided a brief outline of the salmon fishing rights which the townspeople of Selkirk historically enjoyed in respect of the River Ettrick. He explained that during the 19th Century the administration was carried out by Selkirk Burgh Council, however in 1910 the Commissioners for H M Woods, Forests and Land Revenues challenged their right to do so. It is believed they raised concerns relating to poaching, conservation and pollution issues rather than for any monetary gain. In 1912, HM Woods claimed the fishing rights for the Crown and a nominal lease was entered into between Philiphaugh Estates, the Crown Estates and Selkirk Burgh Council for the fishing rights previously exercised by Selkirk Burgh Council combined with those which had been exclusive to Philiphaugh Estates. No major changes were implemented until 1992 when the Crown Estates increased the rental of £85 by a significant amount and continued to do so at varying intervals culminating in the present rental of £4,000 (ex VAT) per annum. As a result of the high fees, membership of Selkirk Angling Association suffered and some members decided to investigate the Crown's claim to the fishing rights.

CONSIDERATION OF CLAIMS TO OWNERSHIP OF SALMON FISHING RIGHTS

3. Sheriff Kevin Drummond introduced himself by explaining that his interest at the meeting was in the legal issues from a community perspective and his attendance was as a private citizen only and not in any judicial capacity. He outlined his understanding of the fishing rights in respect of the following:-

a) The Philiphaugh Estate Stretch - Sheriff Drummond provided further information regarding the history of the salmon fishing rights for this stretch for which he cited evidence to confirm that prior to 1910, Philiphaugh Estate had exclusive rights to fish part of the river and the people of Selkirk exercised rights over the stretch from the Cauld to Linglie March), the administration for the latter having been carried out by Selkirk Burgh Council. *(see map p23 and explanatory note)*. He referred to the lease entered into between H M Woods, Forests and Land Revenues, Philiphaugh Estates and Selkirk Burgh Council following assertion of the Crown Estates' claim. He advised that the terms of the lease clearly state that the arrangement for the Crown Estates to take over control and administration of the salmon fishing rights is "temporary and experimental" only and a copy of the entire correspondence between H M Woods and the agents for Philiphaugh Estates is available in support of this. In addition, a signed Statutory Declaration is also available.

He went on to give details of some brief correspondence in 1925, the preparation of a new lease between Selkirk Burgh Council and the Tweed Commissioners in 1947, to the exclusion of Philiphaugh Estates due to the assumption that the Crown Estates were the proprietors due to the continuation of the temporary lease agreed in 1912. After 21 years, in 1968, Selkirk Angling Association took over administration and has carried on doing so without question until the present. The need to clarify ownership of the fishing rights arose due to the high increases levied by the Crown Estates.

In summary, Sheriff Drummond stated that the issue of ownership of the salmon fishing rights for the River Ettrick had simply been lost sight of over the years and as a matter of law, given the written evidence available, the Crown Estates has no right to ownership. It was confirmed that Philiphaugh Estates no longer wish to take part in the temporary and experimental lease entered into in 1912 and assert their right to re-claim their ownership of the fishing rights.

Mr Jim Drysdale responded that Anderson Strathern have not seen the evidence referred to and would require sight of all relevant documents in order to progress this issue towards a conclusion. It was agreed to provide them.*There followed discussion relating to prescriptive title and investigation of title which the Crown Estates claimed in 1912 they would carry out and Diana Thurston-Smith clarified the position regarding the process for this, however, she advised that the information available to Anderson Strathern is incomplete therefore it is not possible to confirm how the investigation was processed. To assist in this, Mr Graham Philips provided the original HM Woods etc. file number from 1910, S 3627.

It was noted that Selkirk Angling Association under protest, has made payment totalling £8,000 (plus paid VAT) to the Crown Estates, in the past two years.

b) The Selkirk Burgh Stretch – Sheriff Drummond referred to a short stretch of unproductive water the ownership of the rights to which is claimed by the Burgh of Selkirk. In terms of the evidence to support Philiphaugh Estate's claim for ownership of the fishing rights, it was felt that it would be a fitting gesture of recompense if the Crown Estates were to gift their claimed rights on this stretch of water to Selkirk Common Good Fund for the benefit of the town.

Mr Drysdale responded that whilst he could understand why this might be thought an appropriate course of action, he felt that the Crown Estates would not wish to set a precedent for similar requests and suggested that alternatively the Crown Estates may consider selling it to the Burgh of Selkirk following a proper valuation. For the purposes of valuation, it would be helpful if Selkirk Angling Association could provide details of the number of fish caught per annum in that stretch of water.

It was agreed that Anderson Strathern would take instructions regarding this matter.

PROPOSALS FOR RESOLUTION OF DISPUTE

4. In summary, it was proposed

    a) that the Crown Estates acknowledge they have never had proper title to the fishing rights of the River Ettrick

    b) as a gesture of goodwill the Crown Estates were asked to consider gifting their claim to rights on the small, unproductive stretch of water referred to above to the Common Good Fund for the benefit of Selkirk; and

    c) that recompense for the rental paid unduly to the Crown Estates be made.

ACTION FOLLOWING MEETING

It was agreed that prior to any decision by the Crown Estates, a copy of the Statutory Declaration and relevant correspondence referred to during the meeting requires to be made available to Anderson Strathern.

It was further agreed that it would be helpful, but not essential, for Anderson Strathern to have sight of the 'Links in title' for Philiphaugh.

Minute ends.

Contemporary Note: (added by LDN)

Since 1993 to date, Selkirk Angling Association has paid a total of £20,975 + VAT to Crown Estates (total approx. £24,500).

In para 3(a), for clarification, the part of the Philiphaugh stretch in question is upstream of the Selkirk Bridge plus a short length on the North side below the Bridge to a point where it marches with the Linglie. The Selkirk stretch starts from there on the north side and on the south side from the Bridge downwards. Both sides of the Selkirk stretch terminate downstream at Bridgeheugh, with slight differences from the north to the south sides. Selkirk folk freely fished their own stretch and the Philiphaugh stretch upstream to Murray's Cauld, the latter only with the Estate owner's permission. Therefore, in the past, Selkirk Burgh Council did administer the fishings from Murray's Cauld to Bridgeheugh, but only exercised rights on the Selkirk stretch.

Para 3 (b) suggested that renunciation of the Crown's claims would obviate the need for Selkirk openly to argue their ownership case based on the 1159 and 1602 charters, the latter being a barony title with "fishings". It would not constitute an undesirable precedent in view of the previous charters, apparently unavailable to HMW in 1912. Further research by HMW into titles to form the basis of the eventual Oct. 1914 lease would have understandably diminished in importance on account of the more important distractions caused by the outbreak of WW I. The research simply wasn't done.

---

* At her request, a copy of the 1602 charter granting the barony of Selkirk to the Earl of Angus, which specifically included 'fishings', was given to Diana Thurston-Smith. In 1747, in an act of King George II, inherited baronial rights were abolished which meant that Selkirk Burgh fell heir to some of those rights, particularly those concerning fishing. This was further confirmation of Selkirk Burgh's ownership of the fishing rights. (Appendix D)

Comment on the meeting on April 13th

At the meeting AS acknowledged Philiphaugh's title and would arrange to convey it to Philiphaugh. This was a tactic adopted by the CEC to conceal the fact they had never owned the fishings and were now munificently granting the Strang Steel family anew rights the Commission didn't own!

CEC's representatives agreed to consult further on the Selkirk Water and report back. There was a beautiful moment when the Anderson Strathern representatives admitted that they did not have any historical records and correspondence because they had all been lost in the London blitz. We were able to give them both the file reference number for HMW's own file from 1912 and details within it which the Commission knew nothing about. These were from the Glasgow hoard! That was a lovely moment!

The Bridge on the River Ettrick

Unlike the misnamed film 'Bridge on the River Kwai' ('kwai' means 'river' in Thai, so the film title actually says 'Bridge on the River River'), this did involve the removal of a bridge carrying the road over the Ettrick. The one depicted in the film in real life supported a length of track running round a sheer cliff, not a bridge. (Evidence from the late Stan Robertson of Selkirk, a Japanese POW who worked on the infamous Burma Railway on the 'Kwai' and survived.)*

---

*Irrelevant to the bridge collapse, Stan told a lovely story of one incident when he was a POW. He had been in the Border Regiment and was recognised by his fellow inmates as the camp 'fixer', regularly swimming the river to trade with the local Thais, exchanging watches and pens – anything of value – for food. The Japanese commandant decided one day that he wanted a new hut built for himself and the POWs were ordered to build it.

All the POWs were infested with 'mahogany flats', the name given to bed bugs that everyone was tormented by, which were that colour and flat shaped from top to bottom, enabling them to hide in between floorboards and cracks in bamboo huts. Each POW had a matchbox which they all filled with as many mahogany flats as they could find and surreptitiously let them out in the commandant's almost completed hut.

When finished, the commandant was suitably grateful for his new hut and actually managed to sleep in it for two nights before commanding that it be burned down!

The Removal of the Cauld

The Tweed Commission's 1964 intervention and Cauld removal caused alteration to the flow of the Ettrick through Selkirk, destroyed Selkirk's fishing pools and is blamed for sowing the seeds of a later disaster which occurred in 1977.

The justification used was that the Cauld impeded the progress upstream of the spawning salmon.

The Cauld was the property of the people of Selkirk. It had been maintained for more than a century by Selkirk Burgh, with input from the mill owners. Its original purpose was to provide water sufficient to drive mill machinery. Prior to its violent demolition, it was no longer needed as a source of power. However, there had been seven pools in the Selkirk stretch where fish habitually lay and could be caught. After the Cauld's removal, only one pool remained which was only intermittently fishable and from it only about five salmon were caught annually. This was because displaced river gravel/shale was carried into pools obliterating them due to the flow alterations.

Who blew up the Cauld?

The operation to destroy the Cauld was carried out all rather secretly by the Tweed Commissioners with the agreement of Selkirk Town Council. It was done to prevent the local sport of poachers running across the structure, picking up a fish on the way and disappearing into the Bannerfield housing estate before the water bailiffs could catch up with them. Some miscreants had also trained their dogs as poachers and some dogs were very good at it! To the public, it was given out subsequently that it was removed in order to "assist upstream migration of salmon", ostensibly a legitimate responsibility of the Tweed Commissioners.

According to local residents, the Superintendent of the Tweed Commission, a Colonel Ryan, arranged for a detachment of TA Royal Engineers to blow it up. He had previously successfully blown up the Netherdale Cauld in Galashiels. No prior warning was given to the Galashiels folk nor to the Selkirk folk.

Apparently many windows were broken in the resulting explosion. The potentially dangerous operation was completed early on a Sunday morning during the Trades Fortnight which was meant to minimise the disruption but was also when most of the town was away on holiday and therefore unable to protest. The soldiers did as instructed but without any warning being given to those who lived nearby. This cavalier action is still remembered and resented.

So Selkirk lost its valuable fishing stretch with its fishing pools*, and a major tourist attraction to boot. Older members of the community recall weekend busloads coming to Selkirk to watch the salmon leaping the Cauld in the autumn and spring.

The demolition caused a breach in the Could which created a very brisk current through the breach. This in turn caused a swift flow to develop in a previously quiescent section of the river which excoriated the river bank and resulted in a large piece of banking on the northern side to fall into the water. The faster flow rate washed the gravel bed downstream filling the pools and undermining the bridge piers. (Eye witness, Kenneth Herning, member SAA).

The original bridge spanning the river had been built in 1778, designed by Dr. Lawrie, and had been extended and strengthened in the late 1800s. The more rapid flow of water after the Cauld was demolished had a greater damaging effect just downstream of the bridge

---

Another sad result of the Cauld's removal was the end to Dicky Berry's 1960s party trick. Dicky kept horses and was well known as a hirer of them at Selkirk Common Riding. On going home to Bannerfield after a night in the pub, Dicky would jump off the bridge into the water below to impress his friends. One such time he did this and caused a near disaster because he landed on top of local man Norrie Bunyan who was in the act of grabbing a fish underneath the bridge at the time. Norrie protested very noisily apparently. (Norrie was the many hatted habitual cyclist weather predictor who wore up to three hats if it was really cold. Being short and in the habit of scavenging in the rubbish dumpsters, local people soon got to know that you had to make sure you were not dumping stuff on a hidden Norrie. He was often getting dumped on by something!)

than had been the case when the Cauld was in place. The resulting undermining of one of the Bridge piers had not been taken into account at the time of the Cauld's demolition. When the area was later hit by flooding and the Ettrick Water was in spate in 1977, the Bridge collapsed. It cost millions to replace the structure and until a temporary Bailey bridge was assembled, access to the Bannerfield estate — home to some 900 people — involved a traffic detour of several miles from the main part of the town.

It was not long after the upper section of Bridge collapsed that the large portion of the river bank on the north side also collapsed into the river. It had been stable for decades. Luckily no-one was hurt but there was at least one very narrow escape. The late Mrs Bella Hislop was walking to Bannerfield with Pebbles her dog in front of her. The dog sensed the rumbling noise was not good and set off at a fast pace towards Bannerfield. This picture caught the exact moment when the upper part of the Bridge collapsed into the river with Mrs Hislop and Pebbles both clearly seen. Moments later the lower portion followed the upper into the water just after she and the dog had got past.

Concern had been voiced at Selkirk Town Council meeting on July 8th 1964 that the removal of the Cauld might have a harmful effect. More astounding prescience was a report of the Selkirk Burgh Council related in July 16th edition of *The Southern Reporter* which noted that planners had expressed "fears that the breaching of the Selkirk Cauld might result in an extensive movement of gravel, which would affect the stability of the foundations of the piers carrying the road bridge over the Ettrick, especially when the river was in spate". This accurate foresight was voiced by the County Planning Committee and the Town Council was duly warned but paid no heed.

The weakened pier of the Auld Brig was well known to local poachers. The space beneath it and also beneath defects in the Cauld itself were popular hiding places for cleeks and other salmon poachers' implements. Needless to say, the owners of these tools did not inform the authorities that the bridge had been made potentially unsafe.

The Tweed Commissioners were, at this time in the 1960s, the self appointed body of land owners who qualified by owning fishing rights. Their main purpose was to preserve the interests of the owners. They were also bidden to strive to preserve and enhance the salmon population on the Tweed and its tributaries as part of their remit that included the removal of obstructions to the passage of fish spawning upriver.

The Tweed Commissioners, Selkirk Burgh Council and civil engineer contractors all failed to identify risks to the Bridge despite being clearly warned. To them must be attributed

The collapsed Bridge showing the resultant powerful current.

the loss of an old, handsome, Selkirk landmark. The interests and wishes of the Selkirk people appear to have mattered little to them, and their short-sightedness in blowing up the Cauld cost the country an avoidable and very expensive bridge replacement and SAA a fishing venue of considerable value to them.

A sad end to a lovely old bridge and Selkirk landmark.

A delay: what is happening?

We were happy that the Philiphaugh rights would be returned to Philiphaugh but by the end of May, we were impatient to have the matter cleared up with regard to Selkirk and made contact with the Crown Estate. We were also mindful of getting the ownership question settled before the end of the year so that we could reclaim the rental money already paid.

May 28th We arranged for Sir DS to write to IG asking what progress is being made.

May 31st Ian Grant replied stating that "further ambiguities have emerged" to account for the delay without specifying what they were. We had no idea what this meant.

June 24th Sir Robert Clerk from Smiths Gore, a legal firm now apparently representing the Crown Estate, asked to meet at very short notice with David Mitchell and together they walked the river bank. It is now apparent the Crown Estate realise there is a stretch of fishing relating to the Haining Estate and their ownership of that is now mentioned.

The Crown Estates believe they own the Haining fishing rights, and this may be the "ambiguity" that Ian Grant mentions in his letter to Sir David Steel. This had never been mentioned previously but the Commission was now aware that it comprised a part of the fishings leased in 1912.

July 7th To find out what the delay was about, LDN sent a letter to AS asking for an explanation.

July 15th In the absence of a response a further similar letter was emailed.

July 15th Letter from AS to LDN claiming the Crown Estates are considering the situation in the light of Sir Robert Clerk's report to them after his visit to the Ettrick in June. No details are given.

July 15th Letter from CEC to Sir DS saying the same. Sir David also got a letter from the Crown Estates' Rural Customer Services Manager, Fiona Simpson which did not contain any additional information.

Interminable delay

We were now getting a bit fed up and we had acquired a very poor opinion of the CEC both of their motives and their execution.

There appeared to be a deliberate ploy of simply ignoring us. We had already very grudgingly extracted from them, at the Philiphaugh lunch meeting in March, their undertaking to return the Philiphaugh rights to the Estate. In the event this was dressed up as a kind of gift, carefully avoiding any suggestion that their behaviour was anything other than that of a benevolent landlord acting munificently.

We were still waiting for the outcome of a decision over Selkirk's claim and very aware that the deadline that the CEC had unilaterally imposed was drawing near. Our letters and emails went unanswered and we eventually took to sending them by GPO recorded delivery.

Six months had now elapsed from the date of the crucial meeting between the legal representatives of the Crown Estates and the SAA and we were no further forward and no reasons had been given by representatives of the Crown for the hold-up.

October 10th Letter from D Mitchell to AS along lines suggested by KD objecting strongly to their delaying tactics.

November 4th Letter from AS to DM suggesting separate meetings with MSS and S&D AA in Edinburgh.

November 9th Letter from Graham Philips to DM rejecting AS's 'division' of the parties in dispute. All agree to act together and meet in Selkirk, not Edinburgh.

November 22nd Letter from DM to AS rejecting separate meetings and asking for formal replies to letters of 25th July and 21st Oct.

December 9th Short letter from DM to AS requesting a reply to the letter of Nov. 22nd.

Nothing further was heard until finally on 8th January 2006 a request by telephone was made by Sir Robert Clerk for a meeting the following day. Just us, on our own, not a joint meeting.

It had taken nine months and numerous communications to the CEC to evoke a positive response. Not only that but the deadline for the return of overpaid lease money had already passed on the 31st December.

There were no developments over Christmas as we were awaiting a response to our refusal to meet with the Crown Estate's representatives separately from Philiphaugh Estate, and that any meeting should take place in Selkirk rather than Edinburgh.

Then, all of a sudden, after the deadline for the 2005 payment had just passed, the CEC phoned up to ask for a meeting! (*The relevant correspondence is reproduced in Appendix I.*)

The final furlong – 9 months after the meeting in April 2005

2006 January 8th We had received the phone call from Sir Robert Clark (RC) requesting a meeting with the SAA alone on the following day. He had been mentioned in Ian Menzies' letter but collectively we had not met him before. AS and he together had ignored our assertion that Philiphaugh and Selkirk should be present together at any discussions as we were both involved in the same adverse claim. Despite that, they had passed the negotiations to Sir RC without reference to us. We were a little surprised at their tactics. Sir RC said on the phone that he had already arranged to meet Sir MSS separately in spite of our letter. Nevertheless we agreed to meet him the following day.

Note: Whether deliberately or not, a serious and hurried attempt to resolve the outstanding issues was now being embarked upon by the Crown Estate. Significantly it was after the 31st December 2005 deadline, unilaterally imposed by them for return of the 2006 leasing fee, had now passed. We were keen to recover the money erroneously paid.

We believed this to be a deliberate ploy to avoid refunding the money we had paid under protest for the 2006 lease (£4,000 + VAT) coupled with a forlorn belief we would abandon a bid to reclaim our cash after the deadline had passed.

January 9th Dr L D Neil, David Mitchell (Secy SAA) & Alisdair Wilson (Treasurer) met Sir Robert Clerk outside at Philiphaugh Sawmill Salmon Viewing Centre. He proposed to return Selkirk's Water for a one-off sum of £2,500 and rent the Haining Water to SAA for the sum of £2,000 per annum. We thought his proposals were outrageous but said nothing. Sir Robert complained about mounting legal fees and we were delighted to inform him that our legal costs on the other hand were nil. We said we would consider, and respond to, his proposals.

....

Internal Memo by Dr LDN re meeting with Sir Robert Clerk
(Circulated to Sheriff Drummond and SAA members for comment)

[Notes on Meeting between Sir Robert Clark for CEC and David Mitchell, Alisdair Wilson and Lindsay Neil for SAA. Philiphaugh Sawmill 11.45 am 9/1/06]

RC began by saying that on behalf of CEC he had earlier met with Sir Michael Strang Steel and conceded the Philiphaugh fishings. This was breaking news! He said that MSS had said that the Estate didn't want any of the back rent we had paid to the CEC in respect of the Philiphaugh portion paid back to him. *(Confirmed at Appendix J)*

The meeting, which was quite amicable, then went on with RC saying that the case for Selkirk was quite different. He did not concede that Selkirk had title, but was keen to wrap the matter up as soon as possible, and made the following offer.

1. Selkirk water would be returned to Selkirk, title and all, for a one off payment of £2,500. The CEC would take no further part in it.

2. The Haining portion would be leased (anew) to SAA for 5 years at the going rate (based on catches) for £2,000 p.a. (Present lease for all fishings expires 2007)

3. Any arrangement between Philiphaugh and SAA is a matter for them alone.

He confirmed that the CEC claimed prescriptive possession of the Haining stretch and had not been in negotiation at all with the Haining Estate.

He enumerated the problems they had had and said:

1. They had large and mounting legal fees to pay.

2. They were having to account for disposals from the CEC portfolio of properties and therefore couldn't give anything away.

3. They were keen to settle the matter – "it had gone on long enough".

4. They couldn't give things away without complex doings including Royal Assent.

5. They wanted to be friends with us.

We stated that we would consult before any decisions were taken. He would go back to Edinburgh and write a confirmatory letter.

Discussion with RC followed which included us stating that on the evidence we had and the additional evidence gathered from further research, we owned the Selkirk Water anyway. He muttered something about lawyers and their costs and that it was a legal thing that he couldn't pronounce upon – the deal above being the only thing he had to offer.

We ventured the subject of the recovery of overpaid rent and he said that the Philiphaugh portion was between SAA and Philiphaugh, the Haining portion was a non-returnable commercial rent and the Selkirk portion was a tiny amount anyway.

We pointed out that the original agreement stated that rents would be nominal and therefore why was the offered lease on the Haining at commercial rates? He said that the whole deal would be off if we insisted on the nominal rent. He also said that the CE would not give back any money. He said "the Crown Estate don't do that", which the SAA members present witnessed and can verify.

Points: The SAA is having a meeting this Thursday 12th Jan.

RC is reporting to his superiors next day on Friday.

They (the CEC) would like it all agreed by then!!!

The refusal to pay back any money wrongly charged in the past is actually an illegal act under Scots Law.

So, questions to the SAA:

Should we pursue the nominal rent aspect for the Haining?

Should we argue the toss with them re ownership of the Selkirk stretch? (They don't like legal fees!) Or just pay up?

Should we pursue the back rent for the Philiphaugh portion?

Or do we insist on unconditional surrender?

I would favour the following:

a) Say we are prepared to argue the Selkirk stretch ownership.

b) Concede the back rent on Philiphaugh providing they made an ex gratia payment to the repair of Murray's Cauld (the upstream cauld, needing repair badly, and we would have done that anyway).

c) In view of past overcharging that they give us a 50% reduction on the Haining for 5 years.

Honour satisfied, nice undeserved publicity for the generosity of CE, and everybody happy.

What do you think?   **Answer overleaf!**

The SAA when consulted, would not accede to any of the CEC proposals and wished the CEC to be pursued relentlessly. That was unanimous.

January 10th A letter from Sir RC was received, repeating and confirming the CE's proposals as above and stating that no reimbursement would be made. "The Crown Estates don't do that" (said on the 9th) in the presence of witnesses. *(Appendix I)*

The Official Crown Estate's Outrageous Offer

This, therefore, was the Crown Estates' official position and their offer to sell to us what we already owned!

There was no way the SAA would agree to this. The CEC were still maintaining that Selkirk had no right of ownership, were proposing a sale price well beyond the actual value and asked for an exorbitant lease for the Haining. The SAA meeting endorsed pursuit of restoration of total ownership of Selkirk Water.

January 12th Dr LDN, doing more research, finds references in Burgh minutes detailing that the Selkirk Burgh Water was rented out by the Burgh Council in several years, eg. 1802, 1818, 1820 and 1826. This further underlined Selkirk's ownership of the Burgh fishing rights.

Under Scots common law the CEC had undertaken to return the lease charge and had constructed events to overtake the deadline. We reckoned this was pretty devious. They still owed the SAA money!

Reply to Sir Robert Clerk refusing the CE offer.

Jan 15th A letter over LDN's signature but composed largely by KD proposing a compromise settlement taking account of the estimated £12,500 ex VAT overpaid since 1993. Also proposed was that the SAA wanted the abandonment by the CEC of claims to Selkirk Water and also a rational rent for Haining. This approach had been informally approved by the SAA.

The gloves were off, but we were still hopeful of a compromise which would conclude the dispute. I think one can discern a level of legal involvement in the following answering letter given to the CEC!

Dr Lindsay D Neil MB ChB DA

Selkirk, Selkirkshire

Sir Robert Clerk Bt. OBE FRICS

Smiths Gore

12 Bernard Street

Edinburgh EH 6 6PY

15 January 2006

Dear Sir Robert,

Your letter dated 10th January addressed to David Mitchell has been passed to me for attention on behalf of Selkirk & District Angling Association (SAA).

This will of necessity be a lengthy response but I hope that it will give you a clearer understanding of our position and contribute to an early resolution of the outstanding issues between SAA and the Crown Estates Commission (CEC).

First of all may I reciprocate your sentiments concerning our amicable meeting on 10th January at the Philiphaugh Viewing Centre. I agree that it was helpful but the situation as it has now been addressed still leaves a number of important matters unanswered.

Historical Background:

In order to provide some context to this response may I simply remind you of some of the history of this matter.

It was in 1910 that Selkirk Burgh Council first refuted the position subsequently maintained by HM Woods concerning the fishings. Matters were lost sight of on all sides for some time thereafter but following a particularly significant rent increase in 1993 the matter was energetically taken up again by the SAA.

From as early as 1989 and until 2002, inquiries and extensive historical researches were undertaken by SAA. Throughout 2003 various representations were made to the CEC indicating SAA's position. Indeed you may recall meeting with David Mitchell. Notwithstanding that all of our representations were rejected by the CEC we continued with our work because we were confident of our position and this culminated in our intimating a formal claim in November 2003. We had ingathered most of our documentation and were now in a position to lodge a conclusive evidence of our challenge to the CEC's asserted rights.

In the interests of brevity I am deliberately ignoring any reference to the circumstances under which HM Woods and the CEC came to be exercising purported proprietorial rights, but their original basis was not without its problems.

The Progress of the Current Negotiations:

We were initially dealing direct with the CEC who eventually placed the matter in the hands of Anderson Strathern (AS). We corresponded with AS setting out our position which culminated in a meeting at Philiphaugh on 13th April 2005 attended by representatives from Philiphaugh Estate (PE), SAA, Scottish Borders Council and other legal advisors.

The principal, and virtually exclusive, subject matter discussed at that meeting was the status of the Philiphaugh Fishings and, as was plain to all, including AS, that the position of CEC in relation to the PE Water was quite simply untenable.

We fully understood that AS would require to consult further and then advise the CEC and we fully appreciated that that might take a little time.

From May through July and into October 2005 we were writing to AS pressing for a response. When we were informed that you were being brought in to value the fishings on 24th June it was our understanding, rightly or wrongly, that that was the extent of your remit. In the light of the way in which the April meeting had gone, a valuation seemed to be a logical step and represented progress.

By October we were still pressing for progress and a further meeting. Our next information was as late as 4th November when AS intimated that the CEC wished to conduct separate meetings between PE and ourselves. We responded that we were not prepared to agree to that situation but it would appear that the CEC have proceeded on that basis unilaterally. We are not best pleased.

We are now informed by you that the CEC have written to PE intimating that the CEC "have no further interest" in the PE Water. Whilst that is gratifying to hear and is an important part of the position which we have been consistently asserting, it, with respect, does not answer the matters raised at the meeting, nor does it address our adverse claim.

We therefore now assume, (unless the CEC have had a rush of generosity and are gratuitously to be seen to be making over the PE Water to PE) that they have conceded the adverse claim to that extent, which is the only reasonable construction which can be placed upon this development.

This, however, is not wholly reflected in the letter to PE in which it is said that the CEC "have no further interest" in the PE Water.

This representation by the CEC is also said to be conditional upon PE not seeking a claim for past rents received by the CEC.

With respect, the totality of that position fails to address our adverse claim in its entirety and ignores the fact that we have been paying rent under protest for some time on the basis, inter alia, that the CEC had no proprietorial right to the PE Water.

Indeed, by letter dated 17th January 2005 the CEC intimated to us, inter alia, "I am willing to offer a refund limited to the rental due for the year 1 January –31 December 2005 should the submission of appropriate evidence result in a claim being accepted during 2005." The situation for 2004 was in similar terms.

We now find ourselves in a situation where we are addressing new proposals put by yourself which include that there will be no repayment of rent.

It may be that you were unaware of some of the above much abbreviated history. I am sure you will appreciate that the proposals advanced by yourself represents yet another change of position by the CEC.

SAA accordingly finds itself in a position in which it has carefully and candidly prepared its submissions and also which it has exposed to examination by the CEC and its advisors; it has met with them and explored them openly and candidly; its position has been straightforward and consistent throughout. Moreover, it is a position which we have asserted for many years.

The position in which we now find ourselves is accordingly; (i) by letter dated 7th December 2004, both the SAA and the PE adverse claims were rejected, (ii) the CEC now actively seek to isolate our claim from the position of PE, (iii) the CEC now bring in a fresh intermediary, namely yourself, and (iv) fresh proposals are now advanced without the original adverse claim ever being formally concluded.

Like yourself we are anxious to conclude this matter expeditiously and amicably but against the foregoing narrative I trust you will agree that we are entitled to expect CEC to proceed with equal candour in our discussions.

The CEC now accept that they have "no further interest" in the PE Water. That is simply a statement of future interest. It fails to acknowledge the past, the terms of the current lease and our assertion that CEC had no proprietorial right. In addition it seeks to evade any responsibility by obtaining a discharge from PE for past rents and also it pays no regard whatever even to the terms of our current lease.

The conveyancing of the PE Water is a matter which will require to be formalised with PE in order to ensure that this kind of situation does not re-emerge in the future. The position of SAA and PE will, with respect, be resolved for the future between PE and SAA.

The Selkirk Water:

SAA still maintains an adverse claim in respect of the Selkirk Water. Like yourself, we see merit in resolving this whole matter without the need for further complex and potentially extended work on all sides. We are not prepared, however, simply to ignore the history, some of which we have set out above, in relation to the rental paid by SAA to the CEC for the PE Water, particularly with regard to the CE's concession in January 2005 which is now simply ignored in the present proposals and we are told, somewhat high-handedly, that the CEC "will not be repaying any rental". This, we are told is their "policy." The sums involved are significant and we remain prepared to deal with this whole package of issues sensibly but the present proposals still leave a number of matters firmly on the table for resolution.

I suspect that you may be required to acknowledge, perhaps grudgingly, that our extensive researches have produced some pretty impressive material; for present purposes I will say only that there is a great deal more where that came from! *(See pgs 70-71)*

Haining Water:

We know that the Haining stretch is not without its problems. Like yourself we would prefer not to go down that road. In addition, Haining marches with the Cauld. Kendal Fish Farms appear to have responsibility for the Cauld. As you know in recent years the Cauld has sustained substantial damage which may well involve expenditure running to tens of thousands of pounds to repair and for present purposes we make no attempt to analyse the options. Suffice it to say there is potential for serious problems ahead in relation to the Haining water.

We have a position on the matter which we would be happy to discuss.

<u>Our Proposals:</u>

You should also understand that there are strong feelings in the Selkirk community against the community being seen to purchase that which it is believed it already owns. In the circumstances as they are now before us and with goodwill on all sides there is ample scope for the CEC to carry out its own responsibilities whilst being seen to be sensitive to, and having regard for, the interests of the community. We would be happy to assist in facilitating such an outcome. If I may be blunt, on the other hand, SAA in the present circumstances would have no hesitation in instituting proceedings in a simple action for payment. We no longer need the declarator* which we first contemplated.

We will be happy to meet any proposed defence by the CEC, already expressed in writing (more than once), that it is not its "policy" to repay money which it has received and to which it transpires it was not entitled.

That would make interesting reading.

Therefore:

1. CEC have already conceded in writing (January 05) that it will repay certain rents. We hold you to that concession. You offer to sell the Selkirk water; a calculation of the rents involved (even only those already conceded) enables the Selkirk water to be made over to the community without charge by a simple set-off taking account of your valuation. We would not presume to tell the CEC how that would be reflected in their internal

---

A 'Declarator' is a Scottish legal term where the ownership of a property or service can be given judicial integrity by being declared in a court of law.

accounting but we will be happy to co-operate should that be necessary. The handing over of the water to the community can be accompanied by appropriate ritual which would reflect well on the CEC.

2. PE and SAA will enter into a leasing arrangement for the PE water.

3. That leaves only the Haining Water.

   Bearing in mind that it shares water to be fished by SAA and having regard to some of the other matters mentioned above under the heading of Haining and matters as yet unaddressed regarding its future 'fishability', we do not share your views on its value.

   Also taking account of the fact that SAA has been paying rent to the CE for decades for the PE Water, there are a number of imaginative ways in which the Haining Water can be administered to the mutual advantage of the CEC and SAA.

We will be happy to hear from you in early course but it respectfully appears to us that our above proposals have substantial mutual merit which could be explored with advantage at a further meeting.

If you do not find merit in our proposals please let us know frankly and unambiguously. We would assume that any meeting would be taking place on the basis of what we have proposed above.

I look forward to hearing from you without delay. Please bear in mind that the fact that we are in this situation as at January 2006 is attributable wholly to the delays on the part of the CEC.

Yours sincerely.

Dr Lindsay D Neil

(Letter sent recorded delivery 16 Jan 06)

Sir Michael Strang Steel's acknowledgement of the recovery of his fishing rights

January 17th Sir MSS wrote to Sir RC disclaiming interest in past overpaid rent but assigning any interest he may have to the SAA. This is somewhat different to what Sir Robert Clerk led us to believe at the meeting on the 9th and his letter of the 10th. *(Appendix J)*

January 18th Sir RC acknowledges receipt of our letter to him of Jan 15th and said he would seek instructions from the CEC.

Another urgent meeting with Sir Robert Clerk

A meeting requested by Sir RC was again arranged by telephone on the 26th for the following day.

We were now understanding Sir Robert Clerk's modus operandi. He would ignore timetables, undertakings, failed responses by the CEC and by introducing urgency into the negotiations, attempt to wrong foot the SAA. As the SAA had waited months for the CEC to respond, this was rather short-sighted! Our misgivings may not have been entirely his fault! It may be that this was the way the CEC wanted the game played.

January 27th A meeting at LDN's house in Selkirk took place.

Salmon fishing on a stretch of the Ettrick Water near Old Mill Farm.　ⓒ *Walter Baxter, November 2007*

The deal is done!

Selkirk gets its Water back at no charge (to be conveyed to the Selkirk Common Good Fund); a rental was agreed for Haining for five years at £500 p.a. Future rent after five years would be on a commercial basis calculated on catch returns. We asked for and were quoted a price of £84,000 for the outright purchase of the Haining stretch when we proposed it. The purchase of Haining's Water was therefore not proceeded with – we later discovered CEC didn't own that overpriced but valuable asset either!

Minutes of Meeting between Sir Robert Clerk Bt. representing the Crown Estates Commission (CEC) and Selkirk & District Angling Association (SAA) Selkirk. 27 Jan 2006, 3pm

(**Confidential memo** to those named below)

> Present: Sir RC, and Sir David Steel, David Mitchell (Secy., SAA), Alisdair Wilson (Treas. SAA) and Dr Lindsay Neil (SAA researcher)

> Apologies from Sheriff Kevin Drummond QC

The purpose of the meeting was to resolve outstanding matters in the dispute between the CEC and SAA regarding the ownership of fishing rights on the Ettrick and future arrangements for fishing.

1. Sir RC prefaced the discussion by announcing that he was attending with express powers from the chairman of CEC (Scotland) (Ian Grant) to "do a deal".

2. Four areas were identified as outstanding and each was addressed in turn:

   a) Philiphaugh stretch – this was adjudged concluded; the fishing rights being recognised as belonging to Philiphaugh Estate (PE), the CEC had no further part to play and the fishing arrangements henceforward were solely a matter between PE and the SAA.

b) Selkirk stretch – without a formal admission that Selkirk Burgh owned the rights, the CEC would convey the fishing rights to the Selkirk Common Good Fund and renounce any claim to these rights now and in the future. There was to be no monetary sum involved in this transaction.

It was emphasised that the delay in settling the dispute had permitted further evidence to be accumulated by the SAA which provided incontrovertible evidence that Selkirk Burgh did indeed own the rights under barony charters and exclusive possession. *(Appendix D)*

Notwithstanding that, it was accepted that provided a form of wording used in the conveyancing did not dispute Selkirk's right of ownership, this arrangement was agreeable to the SAA.

Note: We were never allowed sight by SBC of the conveyancing documents so we do not know if the CEC stuck to the agreement confirming Selkirk's ownership or instead attempted to purport that they were making a generous gift to Selkirk. We were never able to understand the obstructive, unhelpful and altogether unnecessarily secretive attitude of the Legal Department of Scottish Borders Council. It was their way of doing things.

---

c) Haining stretch – before those present, Sir RC confirmed that the CEC owned title to the fishings of the Haining portion. The SAA accepted that the CEC owned the rights under prescriptive possession and offered to buy the rights from the CEC. While a price was mentioned (£84,000), it was agreed that because of uncertainties over the future 'fishability' of the stretch for several reasons, and because accurate catches for this part of the river have not as yet been compiled, it was difficult to put a realistic valuation on the rights. This avenue was consequently not pursued further. (In fact the value was ridiculously inflated.)

The overall outcome was that it was agreed to terminate the existing lease between CEC and the SAA forthwith and enter into a new lease for the Haining stretch alone at an agreed rental of £500 per annum for five years. At the end of the five years it was agreed that a further lease at a commercial rent would then be offered to the SAA for the stretch, based on the catch returns, as is the normal practice elsewhere.

Sir Robert stated that the leasing charge offered for the Haining was below the commercial rate to take account of the erroneous payments to the CE over the previous 100 years by the SAA.

The SAA would continue to act as caretakers and wardens of the CEC's previously assumed rights, with respect to this stretch, as in the past.

d) Outstanding sums of overpaid rent – it was agreed that the reduced rental charge for the Haining stretch for the duration of the lease and the agreement reached in respect of the Selkirk Water would be treated as an equivalence for the sum claimed by the SAA. It was anticipated that this arrangement would be acceptable to the members of the SAA who would have an opportunity to approve it at the forthcoming AGM of the SAA.

It was recognised that the arrangement still left a sum of £5000 ex VAT outstanding but this sum (out of an approximate total of £12,500 ex VAT), in the interests of avoiding further disharmony and fostering goodwill, would not be pursued further by the SAA.

3. It was identified that the CEC had fishing interests elsewhere in the Tweed Catchment* and it was agreed that the CEC would view sympathetically any proposals for a consortium that might be constituted to safeguard the aims of

---

The Crown Estate also have fishing rights claimed on Gala Water, Leader Water around Earlston, the Teviot at Mansfield Park/Briery Yards in Hawick, on the Tweed itself at Manor Bridge/Neidpath and on the Whiteadder at Paxton.

securing salmon conservation with particular reference to the Philiphaugh Cauld and any other relevant structure, the integrity of which might affect their interests.

4. While it was deemed appropriate for Selkirk to mark the settlement of the dispute by holding some form of ceremony on such an occasion, Sir RC indicated that the CEC had no wish to participate, and this was accepted.

5. A press release would be a necessary accompaniment to the announcement of the settlement at the SAA AGM, however it was agreed that this would be transmitted to the CEC for scrutiny prior to release.

6. A terse typewritten statement on behalf of the CEC announcing the agreement was submitted by Sir RC, to which the SAA had no comment to make.

The meeting was thus concluded with undertakings given by Sir RC to secure the legal paperwork and handshakes all round signified the reaching of an amicable agreement.

....

January 30th: A letter from the CEC (Sir Robert Clerk) confirming the new arrangements was received.

A similar letter from AS to David Mitchell also requesting the name of our solicitor with confirmation of agreement was received.

....

The final letter *(Appendix L)* **– the deal is done!**

Letter confirming that the Selkirk Water rights were returning to Selkirk.

March 8th A letter was subsequently received from Anne Isles (administration and legal department of Scottish Borders Council, administrators of the Selkirk Common Good Fund, SCGF) to LDN requesting confirmation of map showing Burgh stretch. After consulting A. Wilson & D. Mitchell, LDN emailed confirmation.

Conclusion

We could therefore presume that the CE had fulfilled their undertaking to convey legally the fishing rights of the Town Water back to Selkirk Common Good Fund (CGF).

The SAA however were committed to a new rental for the Haining stretch of £500 p.a. + VAT, so from being asked for £4000 + VAT annually, our leasing costs were now much less.

For some reason we did not receive any official confirmation from SBC that the Selkirk CGF had benefited from restoration of what was rightfully theirs. The subsequent efforts by SBC to draw up a nominal lease for a 'generous' £50 p.a. agreed between the SAA and Selkirk CGF was never achieved. Yet the Selkirk CGF was charged a fee of £718.00 for the time and effort SBC spent in attempting a coherent lease. The lease, never having been agreed, has never been paid despite requests from the SAA to formalise it.*

(In 2018, it was finally agreed at the insistence of the SAA.)

A tiny bonus

Somehow – according to the CEC map – we have also acquired a short stretch between the Haining water and the Mauldsheugh part of Philiphaugh fishings. The Crown Estates chart 'pinches' about 50 yards of Selkirk fishing by marking the boundary of the Haining stretch beyond the outflow of the Howden Burn. No action has been taken to highlight this.

The wash-up but not quite the end

Seventeen years after starting to question ownership of the fishing rights – a period of many dramatic twists, turns and setbacks – and having devoted a great deal of time and effort researching and receiving valuable help and cooperation from various local people, we could now at last sit back and bask in the knowledge of a job completed and allow ourselves a small frisson of triumph.

We had recovered properties stolen from the town and from a local estate almost a century ago, and we could now fish unhindered on the Town Water, paying only a small fraction of what it had previously cost the anglers. There were no further disputes: we had simply triumphed in the campaign.

From a leasing charge which had rocketed from £1 to £4,000, we were now having to stump up a mere £500 (+ VAT) annually, Philiphaugh had taken back possession of their Water and so had Selkirk Burgh.

It is perhaps a reflection of a mindset prevalent amongst those charged with administering property alleged to be the property of the Monarch that when this is proven not to be the case and breaches of common law have ensued, an admission of error or guilt is elegantly avoided. Thus it will be recorded for posterity that the CEC generously granted the fishing rights to the Selkirk community and also Philiphaugh Estate as an unalloyed gift of Crown property and not as the final denouement of an act of usurpation perpetrated by their predecessors in office.

The Angling Association was no longer at the mercy of the avaricious Crown Estates which delighted us and we were no longer obliged to spend endless hours examining old charters, documents and histories. It was a pastime which had become a necessity simply because the Crown Estates' forebears had taken it on themselves to ignore centuries-old property rights in 1910 for their own self-serving purposes.

The journey had ended – The Deal was Done - *or so we thought!*

The Haining Story – Phase III begins

The fight for the Haining

Andrew Nimmo-Smith, the owner of the Haining Estate died in July 2009. He had been ill for some time. His will bequeathed the mansion with grounds and a considerable sum of money to the "People of Selkirkshire and the Wider World" in the hopes of it being preserved and not exploited. Before retirement he had been a lawyer practising in Leith. The salmon fishing rights of the Haining Water was a section, 1200 yards long, on one bank of the Ettrick for which the SAA had paid a lease since 1912. It had belonged to the Estate but then had been claimed by the Crown Estate's predecessor, HM Woods, Forests and Land Revenues.

Andrew Nimmo-Smith had deliberately avoided restricting his bequest to the people of Selkirk because Selkirk folk had, in the past, often fished in Haining loch without his express permission. They also helped themselves to firewood from his Estate and because a local councillor had once suggested to him that the Estate would be an ideal site for a crematorium – a suggestion which simply appalled him – he was desperate to avoid this last possibility.

Mr Nimmo-Smith therefore 'took against' the inhabitants of the town. He was also anxious to avoid his Estate land being used as a site for a new housing scheme so his will was framed to avoid that. He acceded to a suggestion made to him in 2006 by the Selkirk Regeneration Group to form a Trust. In the event we were not contacted further but a Trust, as we had suggested, was in his will and was formed after his death. The Group was not invited to participate. He had already sold a piece of land known as Lower Chicken Acre for a housing development. He later much regretted his sale and tried unsuccessfully to buy the land back from the developers who would not sell.

119

After the will was read and understood, a Trust was formed to administer the bequest and the chair was taken by Mrs Susan Edington, the late Mr Nimmo-Smith's lawyer.

The death of Mr Nimmo-Smith inadvertently raised a question over the ownership of the remaining part of the Ettrick for which the Angling Association members were still paying leasing charges to the Crown Estates.

We had already experienced the Crown Estate misrepresenting the true ownership of Philiphaugh's and Selkirk Burgh's fishing rights. They had wrongly declared the fishing rights of the Ettrick unchartered and thus owned by the Crown. They had neglected to establish whether they were right or not despite having promised to do just that. It is unlikely that Mr Nimmo-Smith was aware that he had any fishing rights.

Their behaviour and ultimately their reluctance to relinquish their illegal claim to the rights of Philiphaugh and Selkirk in the face of overwhelming evidence to the contrary made us extremely wary of the CEC's conduct and attitude. So perhaps we did expect to find that, although the Crown Estate claimed to own the rights to the Haining stretch, their ownership claim might well be bogus. To our surprise, that's exactly how it panned out!

2004 - 2009 Relative peace

The Angling Association had not been aware that the Haining Estate had any interest in the Ettrick Fishings in March 2004 when the adverse claim for Selkirk Burgh and Philiphaugh Estate was submitted to the CEC.

We had assumed the Crown Estate owned them because they said so. The only research that we had done was aimed at recovering the Philiphaugh and Selkirk Burgh fishing rights.

When the file of documents and correspondence was discovered in the Glasgow lawyer's office in February 2005, in what we've dubbed 'The Glasgow Miracle', included among the papers was a letter from a Melrose solicitor dated 1912 relating to the Haining fishings. It stated that Mr Pringle-Pattison, then owner of the Haining, in response to enquiries initiated by HMW in 1910, had replied that he "did not claim any right to salmon fishings on the river Ettrick…" *(Appendix N)*

In 2004 we did not know if the CEC knew the Haining fishing rights were separate from the other stretches but decided to keep quiet about it in case they didn't. The CEC, however, after they had abandoned their claim to the other two stretches in March 2006, had 're-discovered' their purported ownership of the Haining fishings that they had first claimed in 1910. The CEC therefore drew up a separate new lease for the SAA commencing from 2006. Initially the SAA paid this leasing charge without protest.

The Haining bequest

When Mr Andrew Nimmo-Smith (AN-S) died in July 2009, he had originally inherited the Haining Estate with the help of his parents who had bought the property for him in 1959. The deed of sale is for 1961 and was a direct disponement from Thomas Place to AN-S.

On his death, the quickly formed Haining Charitable Trust took over the property and his bequest included a fairly run down Estate and a large house needing repair. The Trust was anxious to maximise the income to the Estate in order to maintain and improve it.

On realising that, along with the Estate, the sum bequeathed to "The people of Selkirkshire" in AN-S's will would not be sufficient to sustain the upkeep and development of the property, the SAA decided to look into the ownership of the Haining fishing rights.

If the Haining still owned those rights, any income from the SAA for a fishing lease should rightly go to the Haining and not to the Crown Estate. Our motive therefore was to see if we could augment the funds needed for the upkeep of the bequeathed mansion instead of paying to the Crown Estate.

The doubts as to whether the fishing lease was being correctly paid to the Crown Estate only surfaced when AN-S's lawyer, Susan Edington, mentioned in passing that the Haining was a barony possessed by the late Andrew Nimmo-Smith. Until that moment we had been content to accept the Crown Estate's assertion that they owned the Haining part of Selkirk's fishing lease.

So in 2009 our research started on the status of the Haining barony and the ownership of the fishing rights to the small stretch of one bank of the Ettrick measuring 1200 yards. We had to find and trace the title to the Estate through several transfers to different owners - a 'title trail'.

Ancient barony charters were – as we already knew – nearly always written in Latin. From our point of view the significant inclusion in the charter was the granting of 'piscariis' or 'piscationibus'. It was therefore important to locate early Haining barony manuscripts to see if they displayed references to fishing. If they did then the title to fishings might well belong to the Haining Estate, unless it had been sold off to another owner or, alternatively in the Haining's case, legally transferred to the Crown.

The Haining Estate could only then claim ownership if they had prescriptive possession of the fishing prior to 1910 when the CE first claimed the fishings were 'unchartered' and therefore were owned by the Crown as a regalia minora.* *(See earlier description on page 38)*

CEC's non-repayment of lease money, the date is passed

The meeting called by Sir Robert Clark on 8th January, 2006, had taken place at the Salmon Viewing Centre on Philiphaugh Estate on 9th Jan. [Since the 31st Dec 2005 deadline had passed, the CEC would not, on their unilateral terms, be paying back the leasing charges for 2006.] After ignoring several letters and emails during the whole of 2005, they had waited until early Jan 2006 to call a meeting at one day's notice. This was not an action which enhanced our respect for the CEC. The CEC had deliberately delayed taking any decisions relative to our claim so that a refund of fees for 2006 would not be made on the terms they themselves dictated.

As part of the previous settlement and in view of the CEC returning the fishing rights, the SAA subsequently had agreed not to pursue overpaid lease fees

The CEC, having lost most of their claimed rights on the Ettrick, was still claiming the Haining fishing rights. We needed to do some more work!

More searching

Haining charters until 1870

If we were to be in a position to submit a further adverse claim to the CE, we needed to find original documents to support our case. We searched for Haining charters and discovered two important ones.

Each charter – or foundation writs to use the CEC's terminology – was obtained from the NAS (National Archives of Scotland). Both were barony charters, and they specified that the fishing rights were included with the barony.

The Crown was therefore wrong in stating earlier that the fishings were unchartered and that they could therefore claim them. The Haining fishings were actually chartered. The CEC had no right to claim ownership in 1910/12.

Both charters were in Latin: a charter dated 5 May 1702, from Queen Anne to John Pringle, lawyer, 'legitimate' son of Andrew Pringle confirming his inheritance of the 'Hayning' estate with fishings ("piscationibus") and the free barony of the Hayning. Much space in the charter was devoted to tracing his heritage of the barony title.

The second charter dated 10 December 1754 was from King George II, confirming the barony on John, second son of John Pringle above (who had been in business in Madeira). He was the legitimate heir to his father. The barony is conferred with piscatationibus with the consent of various relatives. So both charters confirmed that the fishings went with the barony title.

A third official document of 17 Jan 1870 proved to be a Deed of Entail* by Anne Pringle-Pattison or Douglas, then inheritor and owner of the Haining. The purpose of this last deed was to legitimise the inheritance of the Estate, prevent selling off and preserve the barony title for the future. In so doing it referred to and confirmed the earlier charters and furthermore that the fishings belonged with the Estate and with the barony title.

It therefore appeared that the Crown Estates, besides not owning the other fishings they claimed in 1912, also did not possess the Haining fishings either. They were the property of the Estate at least until 1870. Until that date, we were able to demonstrate that the Haining had possession of their title by charter.

[Note: We obtained copies of the relevant pages of the Book of the Great Seal from the National Archives relating to the two charters referred to above which were also mentioned as foundation of title in the Deed of Entail. The barony and its fishing assets were thus authenticated.]

While our researches confirmed that the fishing rights were securely with the Estate until 1870, what we could not be sure of was whether the fishing rights were used by anglers from 1870 until the Crown claimed them in 1912. We had to track down the necessary evidence. We needed secure title from 1870 until 1914 and we needed evidence of use of the fishing right during the same period. This was the prescriptive possession.

---

* A Deed of Entail was a legal device occasionally employed and little understood which was entered into by a property owner to secure inheritance to particular named inheritors in writing in order to avoid ambiguity or dispersal of some of the assets on the owner's death. It is now obsolete.

1910 – 1914: The Haining

The CEC by their actions, had cast doubts upon their integrity – or perhaps were simply mistaken. To recap on events so far:

HMW had wrongly laid claim in 1912 to all the salmon fishing rights, Murray's Cauld to Bridgeheugh. Selkirk Burgh and Philiphaugh Estate had both resisted this property grab for four years but to no avail. HMW dismissed all protests despite officially recognising Philiphaugh's ownership in a letter.

An apparent lie was simply that they claimed ownership of something in 1910 that they had already admitted in writing that they didn't own.

They had then stressed that all the proposed arrangements were "temporary and experimental", and claimed the proposed fishing leases were "nominal". HMW undertook to ascertain true ownership of the fishings. A lease from HMW to Selkirk Burgh Council of all the salmon fishings was therefore reluctantly signed six weeks after WWI started in 1914, and was for £5 p.a., negotiated down to £3 by the Burgh Council. We knew about all of their undertakings from the correspondence uncovered in Glasgow.

In 1914, WWI had just started, the sum of £3 p.a. was negligible and HMW having given the aforementioned undertakings, the objections to the Commission's high-handedness faded in the face of world events – and so the lease was signed.

In the case of Haining, the Estate owner had declared no interest, but no conveyance of fishing rights from him to the Crown had been recorded. We conducted an intensive examination of all the relevant Sasines and failed to find that the fishing rights had been transferred or sold. We therefore deduced in retrospect that the Haining fishing rights might still rest with the Estate.

1914 – 2009

There was no real activity during this period in respect of the Haining until it was realised that besides Philiphaugh and Selkirk town fishings, restored to their rightful owners in

2006, the Crown actually didn't own, and therefore had no entitlement to charge rent for, the Haining fishings either. So we embarked on finding the evidence. It meant checking on all the title deeds when the Haining Estate changed hands.

How the Haining changed hands:

1. **10th Nov 1939** – the Haining Estate and barony was sold to Thomas Place by Norman Pringle-Pattison, son of the 1870 owner. The barony and fishing rights had therefore passed seamlessly from father to son before he put them on the market along with the extensive land-holding comprising the Estate. It was subsequently accepted that this conveyance incorporated all the Estate's properties including the salmon fishings.

   In the references to fishings in the original Haining sale particulars of 1939, lot 21 consisted of trout fishing ex adverso* (opposite to) the Haining land bordering the Ettrick. Also, a 15 foot strip of land bordering the Water had been reserved from lot 19 and transferred to lot 21. This enabled the Selkirk and District Angling Association, who also leased the salmon rights on the same stretch of water from the Crown Commissioners, to continue using the trout fishing rights as a separate entity from the salmon rights.

   It also secured to the Estate the right of access to the river bank. Significantly, the salmon fishing rights were not conveyed and ceased to be mentioned after the 1870 Deed of Entail. The lawyer (Mr Turner Dundas) who handled the conveyancing, had failed to register that the salmon rights would have to be separately specified in the conveyance as trout fishing is not a subject for

---

The Provost and Magistrates of Selkirk had purchased 15+ acres of Howdenhaugh (OS 364, part of the original lot 19), bordering the river, from Thomas Place (Sasines June 27 1940) in order to secure extraction of water to serve the town. The strip of 15 ft (above) although contiguous with it, is specifically excluded from the overall estate purchase. This ownership should be researched further as it may still be extant.

conveyancing, being permanently attached to the property's riparian owner. The particular mention of trout fishing therefore implied that the salmon rights had been retained by someone. (The CEC lawyers argued this anyway.)

2. **10th May 1943** – (Sasines 20th May 1943) The barony and lands of the Haining are sold to Mark Fawdry by Thomas Place including the trout fishings and excluding several named properties including those belonging to Lockerbie Savings Bank and the Burgh of Selkirk. Apart from trout fishing, no fishing is mentioned.

3. **22nd December 1947** – (Sasines 23rd Dec 1947) Disponement of barony and lands of Haining by Mark Fawdry to Marjory Katherine Montagu Douglas Scott with exceptions. She was Mrs Pringle-Pattison and was long dead. This entry simply didn't make sense.

4. **5th August 1950** – Disponement by Mark Fawdry to Rodgers (Builders) and marriage contract trustees of Henry Crawford and Annie Ferguson and Donald Fisher – all the lands and the barony of Haining, with eight exceptions including the 15+ acres at Howdenhaugh owned by the Burgh of Selkirk. This conveyance repeated the inclusion of the trout fishing in the Ettrick.

5. **1961** – part of the Haining Estate, the house, land and the barony title is disponed to Andrew J Nimmo-Smith by Rodgers, builders. Only trout fishing is mentioned, and there is again no mention of salmon rights.

2006 – 2009 Lease payments by the SAA

From 2006-2009, the lease was paid to the CEC for the Haining rights without argument or protest. It was still our belief that the CEC owned the Haining fishing rights as Sir Robert Clerk, representing the Crown Estate, had insisted in 2006 that they did.

The SAA had agreed in 2006 to pay an annual leasing charge of £500 +VAT for the Haining fishings and a lease had been drawn up to that effect. The Commission told us this was a reduced cost in recognition of the previous overpayment of the charges on Philiphaugh and Selkirk by the SAA.

We had asked what the outright purchase of the Haining salmon rights would be and were told £84,000. That astronomical figure was one we were not prepared to contemplate. It didn't sound right to us.

It would seem the owners of the Haining Estate during the 20th century had not realised that, as barony title holders, they might also be owners of the salmon fishings. Perhaps the Estate's various proprietors believed the Crown Estates' persistent claim of ownership, and accepted their incorrectly asserted ownership dating from 1912/1914. Like us they did not question the Crown Estates' integrity.

The lack of interest in the Haining fishings by Prof. Seth Pringle-Pattison expressed in a letter to HMW in 1912 gave the Crown a tangible but flimsy excuse that they eagerly seized upon to claim ownership without title. The Crown Estates and their predecessors perpetrated this untruth for over 100 years! But it was not widely known that the Haining was a barony and that Andrew Nimmo-Smith was the Baron of Haining. (He certainly never used the title.)

What was known about the fishing

We told the Haining Trust's lawyer of our belief that the Estate probably owned the fishing rights and not the Crown Estate. The next step was to obtain the permission of the Estate's inheritors for the SAA to investigate the legal ownership of the fishings. This was confirmed by the late Mr Nimmo-Smith's lawyer, Susan Edington, by email.

The confusion over ownership of salmon rights was generated by the professor's letter of 1912 *(Appendix N)*, and was further compounded by the repeatedly erroneous inclusions of trout fishing recorded in successive title deeds from 1939. This mistake was originally made by the solicitor Dundas in Selkirk and was presumably performed through unfamiliarity with fishing law. Separating the trout fishing from the salmon fishing would protect the riparian right of the SAA members as lessees to have access to the narrow 15 ft strip on the river it had owned but the Estate had retained in 1939. But it also unintentionally served to divert attention from the ownership of the salmon rights. It was unnecessary.

Mr Dundas, in drawing up the title transfer from Prof Pringle-Pattison to Thomas Place in 1939, was apparently unaware that trout fishings were not separately heritable and are simply part of riparian ownership. Salmon fishings, on the other hand, have to be specifically transferred as part of a title deed document. This mistake by a lawyer was to cause a major difficulty 75 years later when we were reclaiming the Haining fishing rights for the Estate.

The SAA had all along accepted the CEC's statement that it owned the Haining fishing rights and from 26th January 2006 there has been an agreement between the CEC and SAA which included a leasing charge of £500.00 p.a. + VAT for the now separately identified Haining Fishings.

When it was established the CEC did not own the Haining rights nor any fishing rights on the lower Ettrick, there should have been a sum of at least £12,500 recoverable from the Crown Estates – money erroneously paid to them since 2006 which should rightfully have been collected by the Haining Estate. But when we broached the subject of repayment, Sir RC said at our meeting in March 2006 "the Crown does not pay back money". This was confirmed by letter. *(Appendix I, letter 10th January)*

Summary to 2010 – The SAA refuses to pay lease for 2010/11

Prior to 2006, and since 1914, Selkirk and District Angling Association had paid to the Crown Estates Commission and its predecessors annual lease charges to fish Philiphaugh, Haining and Selkirk Burgh stretches lumped together. These were what the CEC claimed were their Waters.

The sums involved were originally not onerous, and the Haining stretch was not originally separately identified from other fishing rights the CEC claimed. During the 1990s – as explained previously – the CEC greatly increased its financial demands, provoking the investigation which revealed that the CEC were not the rightful owners. It was at this stage the SAA learned that Haining was a barony. Research into the origins of the Estate confirmed the fishings were specified in the title and there was no documentation to show they had ever been sold or transferred to another owner.

The SAA was convinced the Commission did not own the rights and refused to pay the leasing charge. Instead we decided to put the money aside with the intention of eventually handing it over to the Haining Trust if we proved that the CEC didn't own the rights.

Extensive correspondence followed between the SAA and the CEC property managers, Smiths Gore, in the person of their partner Toby Metcalf. He sought legal advice from Anderson Strathern. Their only interest seemed to be in pressing the SAA for payment of the lease regardless of the rights or wrongs of the case.

2011 The questions we needed to ask ourselves and the answers we needed to find

We enumerated the essential questions:

1. *Was the Haining originally a barony, when was it created, and did it still have the title?*

   Yes. The Haining barony was an ancient one and was affirmed in title by charters in 1702 and 1754, by deed of disentail/entail of 1870 and by title dispositions in 1939, 1943, 1950 and 1961. The last (1961) disposition was from Rodgers Builders to Andrew Nimmo-Smith and specifically included the barony title.

2. *Were the fishings specified in the barony title?*

   Yes. The fishings were specified as part of the barony grant in the charters of 1702 and 1754. They were again specified in 1870. The subsequent 1939 disposition refers back to the 1870 deed of entail and its contents, thereby confirming the fishings as part of the barony in 1939. After 1939, the salmon fishings were not mentioned in title deeds.

3. *Were the fishings sold or transferred out of the barony at any time since the charters were granted?*

No. After searching the Sasines, there was no evidence that the fishings were removed from the barony, before or at any time after 1939. All previous and subsequent barony transfers are confirmed as having included the salmon fishings. This is on account of the fishings, when not specified in a narrative barony title transfer, go with the barony title – a legal precedent. (*Ref 8 & 9*)

4. *Were the salmon fishings therefore still included in the Estate title?*

Yes. It would appear so; the claims to own the title to the Haining salmon fishings, asserted by HMW in 1912 and again asserted before four witnesses by Sir Robert Clark on behalf of the CEC on 27th January 2006, were misleading and not founded on any title.

5. *Did the Crown Estates/HMW possess any fishing rights on the Ettrick at any time?*

No. The fishings have remained with the Haining barony title throughout the existence of the barony and are still part of it (see 3 above). They have never been legally owned by the CEC. We had already established that the CEC possessed no title to the Selkirk and Philiphaugh salmon rights in 2006.

6. *Who now possessed the barony title and was therefore entitled to lease the fishings?*

Following the death of Andrew Nimmo-Smith in 2009, the barony title passed to his successors, the trustees of The Haining Estate, subsequently known as the Haining Charitable Trust. They therefore owned the salmon fishing rights and were entitled to lease them.

7. Is the reference to trout fishings relevant to the salmon fishings?

   No. The several references to trout fishings in the title deeds had no relevance at all to the question of salmon fishing rights; the inclusion and reference to them was a simple mistake by the conveyancing lawyer. As described earlier, it is unnecessary for trout fishing to be mentioned in a title deed as it goes with the land bordering a river.

The lawyer's mistake created a Defect in Conveyancing and we were aware that the salmon fishing rights had not been specifically mentioned in the more recent Estate transfers of ownership. Notwithstanding that we were satisfied that the evidence of barony and Estate charters we had provided were sufficient to confirm ownership of the salmon fishings by the Haining Estate.

2012 The Haining Trust submits an adverse claim.

Our evidence was delivered to the Haining Trust lawyer, Mrs Edington.

Armed with these findings an adverse claim was submitted by the Haining Trust to the CEC via their lawyer. It was backed by copies of the various title deeds etc supplied by the SAA. A clear title trail was provided that confirmed the continuity of ownership. The SAA supplied the evidence; the Haining Trust's lawyer, Mrs Susan Edington, was keen to submit the adverse claim in the Estate's name and we had no objection to such an arrangement.

There was little resulting contact with the CEC, but no leasing dues were paid. We assumed they were checking the evidence we'd provided. The leasing charge cash was kept separate within the SAA's accounts and was accumulating year on year.

The adverse claim was submitted by the Haining Trust without informing the SAA that it was done, but must have been sometime in November 2012.

2013 Another delay and the important lunch party

In January, Sir Michael Strang Steel, owner of Philiphaugh Estate and beneficiary of the returned fishing rights, held a lunch party at Philiphaugh. It was attended by Gareth Baird, a Kelso farmer, a member of the Crown Estate board and subsequently in 2015 CEC Commissioner for Scotland. Also a guest was the past owner (Rodgers Builders) of the Haining Estate who had sold it to Andrew Nimmo-Smith in 1961. The purpose was to bring those with interests together in an informal setting.

I explained to Gareth Baird that we had waited a long time to resolve ownership of the fishing rights, we were sure of our facts and could he please attempt to move the issue forward. He promised to look into the matter and into an email sent by us to Smiths Gore. He would see to it that Toby Metcalf of Smiths Gore would be in touch.

We had heard nothing from the CEC or from Mrs Edington so we were unaware that Anderson Strathern had already responded to the adverse claim directly to the Haining Estate lawyer. She had not told us.

[At the lunch, I met the Managing Director of Rodgers Builders, until 1961 riparian owners of the Haining land abutting the Ettrick who remarked: "if we had known about the salmon fishing, we would never have sold the estate with salmon rights to Andrew Nimmo-Smith!"]

A bit of confusion

Because we had agreed that the Haining Trust would submit the adverse claim on their own behalf, we were not the addressees of any replies which all went direct to the Haining's lawyer. Thus we were pressing the CEC for an answer to the claim not knowing that the CEC had promptly answered the claim in December 2012 to Mrs Edington as we had not been informed of the outcome. We had assembled all the documentation for the adverse claim and therefore we were very interested in the outcome.

Finally we did track down a letter from the CEC which we did not receive at the time. It is a mystery where this letter got to.

On further inquiry the Haining lawyer then told us in August that the CEC had sent a letter of rebuttal. This was news to us, so, 10 months after submission, we were able to address the rebuttal!

The Rebuttal of the Haining Claim by the CEC

As delivered to Mrs Edington. *(Appendices O & P)*

The rebuttal had been sent to Mrs Edington but she had not informed us. We felt we were being kept in the dark and didn't know why. At the same time we were pressing the CEC for an answer to our adverse claim and still refusing to pay them the leasing charge they were demanding. Actually, we discovered, there had been some correspondence between the CEC and Mrs Edington. She eventually informed us that she had received a rebuttal from the CEC dated December 2012 but did not tell us this until August 2013. This caused us some embarrassment!

During 2013 we sent many letters to the CEC asking for a reply and getting none. Eventually in 2014 we did get an apology from the CEC for not answering our letters.

We received no apology nor any explanation from Mrs Edington.

In Dec 2012 Mr Jim Drysdale (JD) of AS had written a letter to the Haining Trust rejecting the formal adverse claim submitted by the Trust earlier in 2012. He supplied some inexplicable and confusing reasons for the rebuttal decision. The letter accompanying Mrs Edington's is reproduced. *(Appendix O)*

Although we had supplied Mrs Edington with evidence for submission to the Crown Estates to underpin the adverse claim, we did not receive a copy of what she had submitted nor the date on which it was sent. In particular, we had supplied the relevant evidence demonstrating a continued ownership of the barony title with fishings until 1870 and we had also provided her with a copy of the letter via Curle Erskine from Prof Pringle-Pattison indicating he had no interest in the fishings.

This last was really sent to them to remind the CEC that it did not constitute a legal document and could be ignored as a proof of transfer of ownership. In the event JD used the letter to support the rebuttal.

After pursuing the CEC for months for an answer to our adverse claim: we then got a letter in August from Mrs Edington. *(See Appendix O)*

An enigma – the Haining Trust's lawyer supports the Crown Rebuttal!

Mrs Edington sent a letter in which she stated that she agreed with the Crown Estate's analysis and accepted their contention that the Crown owned the Haining's fishings. She had received the rebuttal from the CEC months previously but had omitted to tell the SAA of her opinion.

It simply made no sense! Who was she acting for? The SAA was performing quite a bit of research on behalf of the Haining Trust without any possible benefit to ourselves in order to assist the Haining Trust finances. There was no clear answer to this enigma and Mrs Edington no longer acts for the Haining Trust.

The Haining rebuttal *(Appendix P)*

In his reply to the adverse claim Mr Drysdale representing the CEC said that he could not accept that the evidence of a barony title with fishings, i.e. salmon fishings, had been continuously held by the Haining barony – although it was plain enough*. He did say it was necessary in addition to prove prescriptive possession in the 40 years from 1870 to 1910 and we could foresee that this could prove difficult.

He also based his rejection on the absence of fishing returns for the Ettrick which he said would have accompanied the returns for Fairnalee which was also owned by the Pringle-Pattisons. He concluded that the absence of catch returns proved that the Haining Estate did not own the fishings because no catch returns were recorded. He also quoted the letter from Curle Erskine (which we ourselves had actually provided from the records found in Glasgow) suggesting this was further proof of the Crown's ownership.

This, in our opinion, was all nonsense!

We were able to point out from our researching that no recorded catches from the Ettrick existed anywhere at that time as the Ettrick beat owners did not submit returns. The tributary of the Ettrick was always in the past considered less important than the Tweed itself for which returns were mandatory. We added that the letter from 1912 from Curle Erskine was simply not a legal act of conveyance. Therefore he was wrong on most counts and not talking sense.

If he was right about the absence of catch returns proving that the Crown owned the rights, then the contiguous salmon beat owners, Lord Polwarth, the Duke of Buccleuch and the Earl of Wemyss and March, should have been subjected to the same claims of ownership by HMW in 1910. From the Tweed Commission's own records which were checked, none of them submitted catch returns for the Ettrick. Needless to say, their ownership was never challenged. Only the owners of property without hereditary titles were being challenged – underlining the prevalent class distinction mindset.

However, under strict interpretation of the law we were left with having to prove prescriptive possession and in referring to that Mr Drysdale was correct. We therefore set about trying

---

It was established by legal precedent (LA vs McCulloch; 1875, 2R 27) that it was unnecessary to specify that salmon fishing went with the remaining property when a barony ownership was transferred. It was accepted that 'regalia minora' could be included with title, even if unsaid, but that prescriptive possession had to be proven. Mr Drysdale should have known this. His assertion that the fishing did not go with title was therefore mistaken. He was not supported by the law. Ref 38, SLT 1875.

to find legally acceptable evidence that Selkirk people fished on the Haining stretch of the river between 1870 and 1910. We ignored the other conclusions arrived at by Mr Drysdale as irrelevant. This alone was going to be a nearly impossible task!

We were utterly stunned by Mrs Edington's unexplained agreement with the CE's decision to rebut the adverse claim. We asked for her reasons in legal terms, but did not receive them and they were never explained. Our respect for her legal opinion took a big hit as a result! When we had presented her with the SAA's opinion that the decision was unfounded on fact, Mrs Edington suggested hiring another QC to settle the issue. As we already had a QC opinion, we rejected such a ridiculous idea as simply a waste of scarce Haining Trust money. We needed to bypass the Haining Trust's lawyer!

The SAA had written to the CEC on several occasions between August and November 2013 and received no reply. Finally, Sir David Steel wrote in December 2013 on behalf of the Association to Alison Nimmo, Chief Executive of CEC, asking what progress was being made towards resolving the Haining issues and why our many letters had remained so rudely unanswered. He received an apologetic reply suggesting a meeting to try to resolve matters.

As explained earlier, the leasing charges for 2012 and 2013 were separated from the normal SAA accounts with a view to paying them to the Haining Trust, the rightful owners, if we were proved right, or eventually to the CEC if we were found to be wrong.

This decision had been intimated to Toby Metcalf of Smiths Gore, representing yet another firm of lawyers as well as Anderson Strathern representing the CEC to whom we had also written. Mr Metcalf seemed only anxious that we paid our lease and took no account of the rights and wrongs of the situation. If we did not pay up he warned we "would be fishing illegally".

We considered his demand and threat were laughable and planned that, if necessary, all the SAA members would simply turn up and openly fish in the Ettrick. Simultaneously we would inform the police officially and the press that we were doing so (allegedly illegally), confident that the embarrassment to the CEC would preclude them from taking any action.

In the event, Toby Metcalf arranged a meeting between the Association and the CEC's lawyers, Anderson Strathern, and we readily agreed to this. At last some progress was being made!

....

Anderson Strathern participate

2014 Meeting with the lawyer representing the CEC

The meeting was held in Selkirk on 3rd March.

Those present were: Anne Chapman, a lawyer from Anderson Strathern, Toby Metcalf from Smiths Gore and David Mitchell, Adam Borwick, Kevin Drummond and Lindsay Neil from the SAA. Anne Chapman whom we had not met before was refreshingly clear, direct and straightforward. Mrs Edington, the lawyer for the Haining Trust, was not present.

A limited tour through the history of the dispute was led by KD and subsequent discussion resulted in a number of conclusions being arrived at, enunciated by AC.

1. The early charter of the Haining barony was accepted, but while fishings were mentioned it was not specified that this applied to salmon (Green's Encyclopaedia of Scots Law disputes this view, but we did not argue).

2. The flawed legal work of 1939 (failing to mention salmon fishing) needed a remedy. It was accepted that this represented a defect of conveyancing and it had been intended that salmon fishings accompanied the barony in all the Estate ownership transfers post 1939.

3. While the 1910 declaration by William Strang Steel (endorsed in 1912 by his son Samuel) confirmed that he permitted his Water to be unrestrictedly fished prior to 1910 was acceptable as sufficient evidence of prescriptive possession for Philiphaugh, it was not considered by the CEC that it applied equally to the Haining side of the same river in the same place. We disputed this. However,

prescriptive use, i.e. evidence of possession/use separately by the Haining Estate prior to 1914 was insisted upon by the CEC, otherwise they would exercise their superior right and claim the fishings.

AC concluded that in order to substantiate a claim on the fishing rights, the SAA must:

a) Cure the defect in conveyance; this, it was accepted, could be achieved by registering an a non domino (AND) title on the fishings covering the period from 1939 to the present, asserting that the salmon fishings were erroneously excluded from the relevant deeds.

b) Prove prescriptive possession by the Haining Estate between 1870 (deed of entail) and 1912 when HMW assumed ownership of the fishing rights. In other words, show that salmon fishing was practised freely by local people within the law and without interference from the Estate – "…openly, peaceably and without judicial interruption."

If that was all done, the adverse claim would be accepted and the fishing rights would be transferred back into the possession of the Haining barony.

It was agreed that the Haining Trust's lawyer would submit the AND title claim and that the SAA would do further research to find evidence of fishing between 1870 and 1914 in order to confirm the Haining's prescriptive possession.

The QLTR and an a non domino* title

There was therefore going to be an accepted clear title trail of fishing rights of the Estate and barony from the Pringle-Pattisons to Andrew Nimmo-Smith (1939 – 2009). The salmon fishing rights had been regrettably overlooked and omitted from the title deeds during that

---

* a non domino *'A Non Domino' means literally 'from the non-owner' and is a handy legal device to allow the granting of a title to property to someone else by someone who doesn't own the property. Usually it is where a title deed is missing or incorrect. It can't be from one person to him/herself.*

period. Therefore what was absent was a continuous conveyance of the salmon fishing rights between 1939 and 2009 which had to be 'cured' by the submission of an a non domino application for the period to the QLTR (Queen's and Lord Treasurer's Remembrancer). The QLTR was the Crown's representative who accepted ownership on the Crown's behalf of any property for which no owner could be found.

This was done by Mrs Edington, the Haining Trust's lawyer, on their behalf. It was pretty straightforward because the CEC accepted that there had simply been an error of conveyancing which needed to be corrected to confirm the Haining's ownership. Mrs Edington did not confirm that this had been done but we did get confirmation by other means.

The question of establishing prescriptive possession for the period was not considered a necessary condition and the QLTR accepted the application. (We were not copied in to the correspondence but the success of the application was assumed.)

Our task now? More research to identify prescriptive possession*

Because the CEC insisted on evidence of prescriptive possession we then undertook painstaking scrutiny of all the Tweed Commissioner's records. Catch returns for the Ettrick were very sparse, we investigated valuation rolls, and also neighbouring estates' records, Our search also covered Selkirk Burgh records back to 1800.

We made appeals to the local press, and a search for any source that might throw light on how the fishing was carried out in the critical period 1870-1914. All these searches were fruitless, there was no historical record of fishing in the Ettrick although plenty of records of angling in the Tweed.

---

prescriptive possession The Haining Trust had submitted an a non domino title application, and we were confidant from assurances given that that had been done. We now had the more difficult task to deliver to the CEC the proof of unhampered fishing during the critical period. We had to prove the use of the title by someone fishing between 1870 and 1912 which was more than just hearsay. There had to be hard evidence.

It was simply the case that no systematic records were kept for the catches from the Ettrick although references to catches, of no value to us, were occasionally made.

From our past dealings with the CEC we were perfectly willing to believe that this condition was deliberately imposed on us in the belief that we would be unsuccessful and the rights would then pass to the Crown.

Having got this far, we were not going to leave any stones unturned in our searches!

Another miracle – this time the Haining

Amongst the many potential sources we researched exhaustively, one was a simple enquiry made to the National Archives of Scotland (NAS). The NAS told us it had something relevant and would send it for a fee. We paid up, but it turned out that the NAS did not have the item promised as they had already lent it to someone else. They told us it was a newspaper cutting, and it had gone to the Crown Estate who now had it. Further enquiries revealed the cutting had been passed by the CEC to Anderson Strathern, their lawyers. When contacted, AS agreed they had the document and readily agreed to send us a photocopy. It may be that they thought providing us with something that was not within the period 1870 -1912 that their case would not be harmed. The NAS, an honourable organisation, sent the fee back!

The article was from the Daily Mirror of 1913 and contained several photographs of fishing activity in the Ettrick and all photographs bore a number. This was the only piece of evidence that we had turned up so was worth pursuing even though 1913 was outside the critical period. One of these poor quality photos (no. 5) depicted a bearded man handling a salmon, the caption read "one of the oldest anglers on the river".

We arranged for copies of the Daily Mirror photographs to be published in two local papers, The Border Telegraph and the Selkirk Weekend Advertiser, and asked if readers recognised anyone in the pictures and if so could they get in touch.

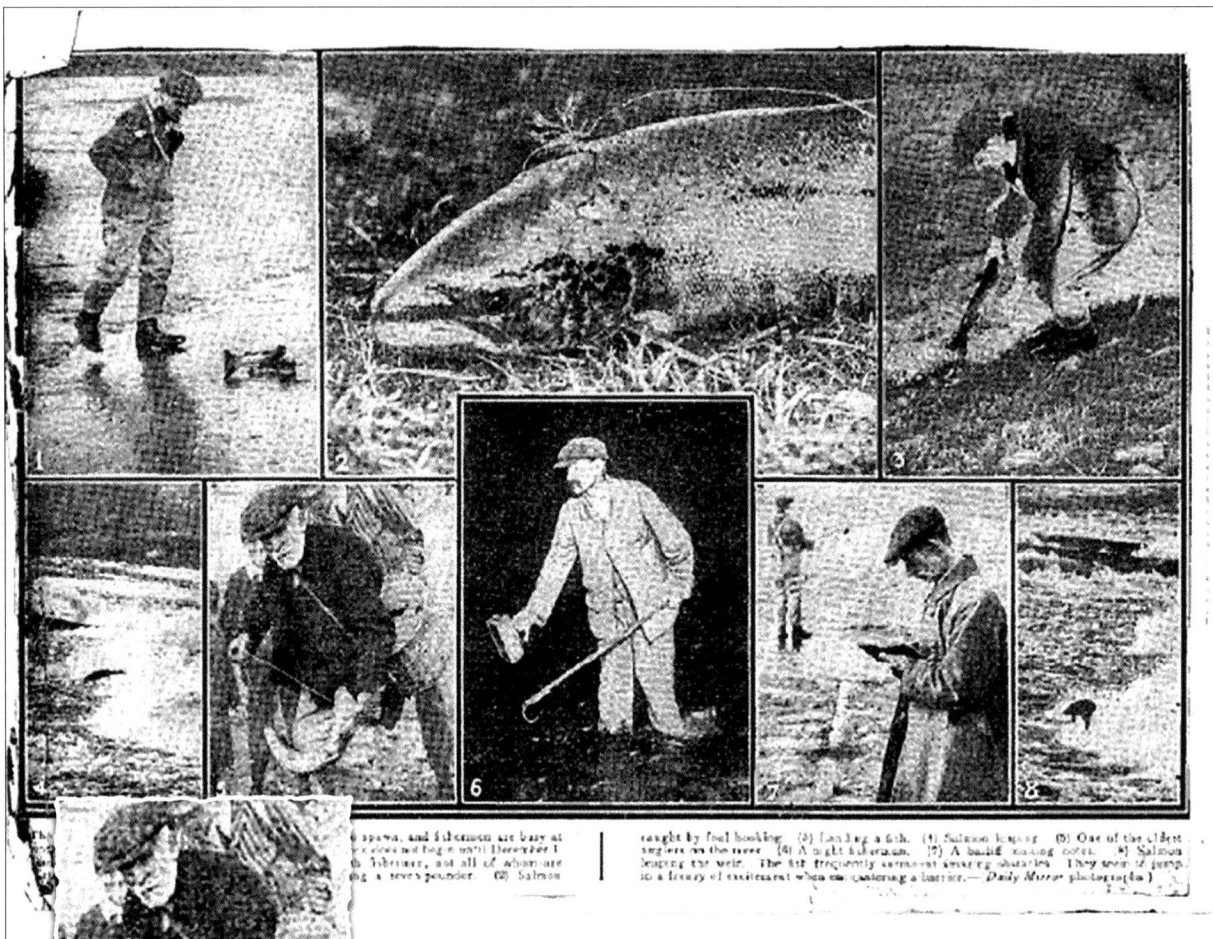

To our utter amazement, a Mr Ian Hope from Selkirk phoned to say that he immediately recognised his Great Grandfather, Bertram (Bat) Tyson and he had another picture of him which he showed us. It was unmistakeably the same man!

Bat Tyson to the rescue

Bat Tyson proved to be a notorious individual. As this was the only lead we had, it was important to research his fishing activities to see if they could throw any light on what happened in the late 19th century with regard to fishing. What we discovered was astonishing and provided us with all the evidence and more than we needed to prove prescription.

Bat Tyson photographed by the Ettrick Riverside in the early 20th Century   (Courtesy of Mr Ian Hope)

About Bertram (Bat) Tyson

Born in Selkirk in 1854 Bertram was a mill and dye house worker for all of his working life. He died on 11th Sept. 1928, at 16 South Port aged 74. He is recorded as having lived at 17 Dunsdale Haugh in the 1901 census; at 19 Kirkwynd in the 1911 one, and had also lived in Anderson Road at some point. All of these addresses were in Selkirk.

He was a renowned and keen fisherman and a popular personality. He married in 1881 in Buccleuch Road, Selkirk, to Joan (Nichol). Between them they had four sons and five daughters.

Three sons were sadly killed in various actions in WWI. Their names appear on the Selkirk War Memorial. The family descendants believed they were all killed on the same day in the same place but we found that the dates and places were widespread.

Bat was 47 years old in 1901 (1901 Census), therefore about 59 in the 1913 Daily Mirror photograph.

His living relatives are: great grand-daughter, June Pringle of Newstead; great grandson Ian Hope, brother of above, Selkirk; cousin of both the above, also a great grandson, Alan Davidson of Lamancha, near Peebles.

Bat Tyson and Joan Tyson (Nichol) wedding day 1881. Bat had been a colourful character and had had several scrapes with the law.
(courtesy of Alan Davidson)

144

Bat's fishing successes and trophies won:

1887 Won 3rd prize in the annual Selkirk Angling Association fishing competition.

1888 Won 1st prize in the next annual competition.

1889 Won 5th prize in this year but also 1st prize for heaviest ½ dozen fish.

Sources: Southern Reporter 1887, 88 & 89; 1892 and 93. Edinburgh Evening News 5/8/1889.

Bat Tyson: significant dates and court appearances

1873 27 November – Guilty of trespassing in pursuit of game – fined.

1887 21 July – 3rd prize in annual Ettrick fishing competition.

1888 26 April – 1st prize in annual Ettrick fishing competition.

12 July – handicap competition; trout in Tweed, Ettrick, Yarrow & Meggat, he came 4th.

1889 8 August – 5th prize in annual fishing comp. Also heaviest ½ dozen trout.

1891 15 January – Guilty of 'raking' near Lindean Bridge – fined.

29 October – Along with others, engaged in a fracas in Bridge Street – fined.

1892 15 December – Accused of 'sniggling' and being in possession of illegally caught fish. Found guilty by the sheriff and went to prison. Manifest miscarriage.

22 December – Spontaneous public meeting protesting wrongful imprisonment.

1893 16 February – Thomas Shaw, MP for the Border Burghs, asks questions of the Scottish Secretary in the House of Commons re the Tyson case.

1894 27 September – Victim of assault in Amos' Eating House in West Port by Robt. Heard who was fined for the offence.

1895	14 February – Guilty of stealing coal. Sentenced to 10 days jail.
	19 September – Guilty of failing to clean passage in Dunsdalehaugh. Admonished.
	23 November – Fishing illegally. (Six previous convictions noted.) Fined.
1896	22 October – Together with his wife, guilty of Breach of the Peace. Fined.
1901	17 October – Fight in Station Hotel reported to court; 24/10 – Accused of fighting over 3d during a game of dominoes in the hotel. Fined 5/-.
	10 December – with brother George and son Hugh, found in possession of a 'straking net'. Fined, Hugh let off.
	12 December – Appears as a witness in a case against a water bailiff.
1903	1 January – Acted as a witness in an assault case.
	15 January – Was witness to Mr Gilhooley's breaking of windows, who was found guilty at trial.
	5 November – Assaulted by Peter Park in the Queen's Head Inn during a game of dominoes.
	10 December – Fined 20/- for Breach of the Peace in Back Row.
1920	Bat's three sons, Bertram (HLI), James (A&SH) and John (KOSB) all killed in WW I, are mentioned in the Selkirk Roll of Honour. 30/9/1920
1926	5 August – Bat accuses a water bailiff of assault. Case 'not proven'.
1927	21 July – Apprehended with a rake at Philiphaugh Cauld and also accused of threatening to knife the bailiff. Fined.
1928	11 September – Died at 16 South Port. (Family story is that he was assaulted by a bailiff who delivered a head injury, ultimately fatal. (Bat refused to inform the police.). He was therefore most likely murdered by his assailant.

[Source: British Newspaper Archives, mainly Southern Reporter]

The Case that Changed the Law

The important historical record holding the answers we were seeking concerned events which occurred in November/December 1892. The date was slap bang in the middle of the period during which we wished to prove prescriptive possession existed. Bat and his brother George were unjustly accused of illegal possession of salmon at Selkirk railway station and also faced charges of illegal fishing. They were both later convicted.

Bat's popularity in the town was confirmed by the speed with which a public meeting was called in December 1892. They objected to a "perceived miscarriage of justice and the manifest unfairness of the law". Astoundingly, the meeting was held only a week after their court appearance.

The subsequent representation of Bat's case was when a question was raised in the House of Commons by the local MP which led to the eventual amendment (1911) of unjust clauses in the Tweed Fisheries (Scotland) Act of 1857 and 1859. These acts, uniquely, stated that where an individual was accused of breaching the terms of the act, **guilt was assumed** unless the accused was able to prove his own innocence.

The law was changed!

One may comment that it took almost twenty years for Parliament to amend a legal anomaly after it was publicly and clearly identified. This one small area of law allowed an accused to be presumed guilty until he himself laboured, probably held in custody, to prove his own innocence. The beneficiaries of any fines levied were the parish and the owners of the fishing rights in the form of the Tweed Commissioners. The Tweed Commissioners in 1892 were self appointed and, along with the water bailiffs, had a financial interest in convicting as many individuals as possible. It was stated in court that the parish hadn't ever been given any portion of the fines levied although the act dictated that they were entitled to a half share.

Note on the Tweed Commissioners

In 1771 the Tory Government under Lord North introduced a bill to "regulate and improve" the fishing on the Tweed. This was in the same year as Ben Nevis was first reported climbed; Captain Cook had set sail for the South Seas to 'discover' Australia and New Zealand, and the Falkland Islands were ceded to Great Britain by Spain.

The intention of the 1771 Act was to protect the spawning fish and a closed season was first introduced from Michaelmas (29th September) to Candlemas (2nd February). As alluded to earlier, huge volumes of salmon were being caught by nets at the mouth of the Tweed and thereby being prevented from spawning. The original act was simply ignored by the lower Tweed owners and had to be amended in a further act in 1775. The close season was changed to 10th October – 10th January.

Anyone caught illegally fishing for salmon during those times would suffer financial penalties, half of it given to the informer or witness, the other half to the parish.

The Berwick fishermen and those as far upstream as Kelso were dissatisfied with the curtailment of their lucrative industry and held a meeting in 1773 and again in 1781, this time forming an association. The situation still needed sorting out; disputes were common, the previous closed seasons continued to be largely ignored and so a further act was passed in 1805.

The owners of fishings upstream of Kelso were not included in the original Berwick association and in 1805 formed themselves into a separate body. The new group declared that the "object of this association being only to secure the just rights of the members". The new 1805 Act was not based on these associations that had just been formed but rather on the basis to benefit those who owned fishing rights. Responsibility for regulation was devolved to the individual owners.

This latest legislation act was to strengthen the previous Acts and define a legal framework.

Commissioners and overseers were mentioned in the act but their role was not defined. They therefore had no status as law enforcers.

The Berwick committee and the newly formed Upper Tweed Association eventually agreed to amalgamate and had original members including Lord Somerville, the Earl of Dalkeith, Sir Henry Hay MacDougall, the Sheriff of Selkirkshire Sir Walter Scott and, in essence, those with land or titles. They called themselves the Tweed Commissioners but did not receive official legal recognition as such until the River Tweed Order of 2006. Until 2006 they were simply a self-appointed private association.

The Tweed Commissioners framed their own rules more or less as they pleased. When Bat Tyson's wrongful imprisonment took place in 1892, their prejudicial and unjust adherence to these bad laws eventually led to a change.

The owners were presented with various agreed areas to monitor and set about it. The most important measures introduced to regulate their new responsibilities were:

1. The observance of the closed season so that the fish had a chance to swim upstream to spawn unmolested.

2. The securing of free flow of fish through caulds and traps.

3. The appointment of a qualified lawyer (Erskine of Kelso) to act as their agent.

4. The appointment of water bailiffs. (There were 47 in 1807 plus a further 11 who were paid a retaining sum.)

5. The prevention of poaching and the prosecution of poachers.

6. To procure rental of fishing for the owners and to hold an annual meeting.

It is important to note that one of the principal aims of the association was to secure profits from their ownership of fisheries. Their assumption of quasi-legal rights by the employment of bailiffs as enforcers of the law was naturally unpopular amongst anglers.

There was also the agreed principle that bailiffs received half of any fine and the other half was paid to the parish. This was therefore an incentive to enhance the volume of convictions which was to have significant implications later in relation to the Ettrick. These were not generally seen by the public as generous arrangements. There has been no record found that the parish ever received anything.

The 2006 Order changed the scene; not only were police officers given the rights previously enjoyed by the water bailiffs but the bailiffs' powers were radically curtailed. The River Tweed Commissioners were at last recognised officially and were no longer a private body although still had a membership largely restricted to owners. In addition, they no longer profited from successful prosecutions and had limited powers otherwise. Water bailiffs were appointed by the now recognised Tweed Commissioners but could only act in concert with the police.

Significantly, the Commissioners no longer had a role in protecting the interests of the owners but their legal role was now only to promote the wellbeing of the fishing stocks and monitor the quality of the river.

The Tyson Case at Selkirk Sheriff Court

On November 15th, 1892 Bat Tyson and his brother George were accused by a water bailiff (a Mr Inglis) of being in possession of illegally caught salmon on Selkirk railway station. During the court case held before a notoriously harsh sheriff named Harper, several points were made in court in defence of the Tysons:

1. Both had, during the permitted season, claimed to have been fishing all day legally with rod and line at a point 30 yards below Philiphaugh Cauld on the November day in question.

2. A witness gave evidence that he saw them fishing with rod and line from his position on the opposite bank, where he was likewise fishing, and confirmed the defendants' evidence. He had watched them catching a fish. (This piece of

witness evidence is crucial as one or other, either the witness or the accused, was fishing from the Haining-owned beat.) This evidence was ignored.

3. It was stated in court, and not disputed by the prosecution or the sheriff, that fishing for salmon with rod and line was perfectly legal in this location at that time of year.

4. No evidence was presented to show the defendants had been observed fishing illegally by the bailiff or by any other person.

5. The fish discovered at Selkirk Station, in a basket assumed to be owned by Bat Tyson, contained two salmon, five sea trout and three brown trout. George Tyson did not admit to owning them and they were not proven to belong to him. He should therefore have been discharged. Bat Tyson on the other hand admitted he owned the fish.

6. One fish had a minor mark on its side, possibly caused by a hook or illegal instrument according to the prosecution. Other witnesses attested the marks could have had no significance in view of their own experience of catching similarly marked fish and therefore not evidence of illegal sniggling (trawling a pool with a weighted line with multiple hooks thrown across the river). Nor was it evidence of raking or cleeking.

7. The bailiff had failed to examine the mouths of the fish in order to find any hook damage which would have confirmed the defendants' submission. The bailiff's accusation was based purely on a supposition that the fish had been caught illegally and not by rod, line and hook and that their possession was illegal.

8. The acts under which the charges were being brought were the Tweed Acts of 1857 and 1859. These acts empowered the self-styled Tweed Commissioners to act in a legitimate but in an unacceptable manner.

Importantly, and uniquely under the acts, the accused was presumed to be guilty until he was able to prove his own innocence. The defence recorded that Lord Young, a Scottish judge in a previous judgement, had deemed this to be virtually impossible in angling circumstances.

Water bailiffs appointed by the Tweed Commissioners were not required to have any qualifications and many of them had no knowledge or experience of fishing. In those days any Tom, Dick or Harry would do.

The Sheriff's decision and misapplication of the law

Sheriff Harper in disregarding most of the evidence given in court -

- Decided that the fish belonged to both the Tysons.

- Decided that illegal fishing was proved by the mark on one fish and in view of each having had previous convictions under the acts, found them guilty; he also said that the accused had failed to prove their innocence as dictated by the acts.

- Disregarded the evidence that the fish were witnessed being **legally** caught with rod and line **at a location below Philiphaugh Cauld.**

- Disregarded that, under the law, fish could be legally possessed by anyone.

- Found the brothers guilty of illegal possession and illegal fishing.

- Fined them £10 or three weeks in prison. (They chose prison.)

- Refused an appeal on technical grounds which were never specified.

Public meeting of protest

One week later, in view of the high regard that Bat Tyson and his brother were held in Selkirk and in commendable recognition of an injustice, a public protest meeting was held in Selkirk Volunteer Hall on the 14th December. It was attended by local notables and an ex-MP. The meeting's purpose was "to protest the harsh and oppressive elements of the Tweed Fishery Laws". The Tweed Fishery Reform League, an existing protest group, arranged the meeting and acted as host.

During the meeting it was said :

i) There was not "a rag of evidence" that the brothers had been fishing at all on the day in question between 11am and 7pm.

ii) There was no evidence to connect George Tyson with the fish in the basket which had belonged to his brother who admitted ownership. He should therefore have been discharged.

iii) Possession of fish at that time of the year was, in any case, not illegal.

iv) The Tweed regulations were obnoxious and brought the law into disrepute.

v) Poaching was deprecated but the laws did nothing to discourage it.

vi) The Sheriff was respected but had veered from sensible law.

vii) Any statute which assumed that an accused was guilty until proved innocent was singularly unjust and contrary to existing common law.

viii) The fines levied by Sheriff Harper were much too heavy.

ix) The Tweed Commissioners had been "impertinent" and were ridiculed for requesting a Man o' War to be sailed north to the mouth of the

Tweed to protect their fishing interests. Equally ridiculous was the suggestion attributed to the Tweed Commissioners that a Company of Militia be stationed at Lindean to discourage poaching.

x) Those who called themselves Tweed Commissioners were simply self-appointed river proprietors with monstrous powers.

xi) Bailiffs could be of no reputable character and were qualified for the job simply by being unemployed at the time.

xii) Any money raised from fines imposed under the acts was given directly to the Tweed Commissioners who therefore had an incentive to maximise convictions. The fine money was supposed to be divided equally between bailiffs and the parish.

It was decided to write to prominent politicians including the Scottish Secretary and the Prime Minister to protest the acts and the outcome of the case. Meanwhile, Bat and his brother served their sentences.

Question raised in the House of Commons

On 16th February 1893, Mr Thomas Shaw, MP for Hawick, asked a question on the Tyson case and received a response from Sir George Trevelyan, Secretary for Scotland. *(Appendix R)*

The exchange is preserved in Hansard, the official record of Parliamentary proceedings.

National conclusions and outcome

It was agreed at the highest levels that the Tyson brothers, due to the application of an unjust law, were convicted of an offence which was not proven. The law in this case was defective and the River Tweed Fishery Laws were draconian, in need of amendment and were framed in a manner contrary to normal justice where innocence prevails until guilt is established.

The period during which the Tyson trial took place was not alone in turning what we would nowadays regard as normal justice on its head.

In the years leading up to the eventual legal enshrinement of the principle that an accused is innocent until proved guilty, various miscarriages of justice took place. A notable one was where the judge encouraged the jury to convict a man because he was Jewish and had not proven himself innocent. This was the celebrated murder trial of Oscar Slater. He was being tried for murder and robbery in 1909, and was found guilty on the direction of the Judge Lord Guthrie. There were numerous defects in the prosecutions case but the judge advised the jury to convict and Mr Slater was condemned to death. He was reprieved 36 hours before execution but still spent 18 years of hard labour in Peterhead prison under a commuted life sentence.

Discharged in 1927 he died in 1948 but the widespread realisation that he had been wrongly convicted resulted in the universal law which became that an accused was innocent until proved guilty. It was also changed in the amendment to the Tweed Fisheries Act in 1911. Perhaps this case hastened the enactment of a change in the law which, had it been extant in 1892, would have exonerated Bat Tyson. An innovative Court of Appeal was instituted in the same year.

Extracted from:

Southern Reporter, 15/12/1892

Tweed Fishery (Amendments) Act 1857 & 1859, Sections 6 & 10.

Southern Reporter, 22/12/1892

Proving prescription

The Selkirk and District Angling association and the Haining Charitable Trust have good reason to be grateful to the officious Mr Inglis, the accuser of the Tyson Brothers, to Sheriff Harper for his unwavering determination to ignore evidence and to apply the law irrespective of justice; to the British Government for enacting and condoning laws that turned justice on its head and to the River Tweed Commissioners for being so arrogantly set on the pursuit of even small sums of money regardless of justice.

Between them these actions and inactions collectively contributed to the righting of several wrongs, the belated recognition of justice in this small area of Fishing Law and the ultimate restoration of property to the Haining Barony. 100 years later, it also settled the question of who owned the fishing rights wrongly claimed by the Crown.

In respect of the Haining, it has to be said that immense credit is due to the citizens of Selkirk who, despite the sizeable record of Bat Tyson's minor crimes and previous poaching habits, recognised instantly that a flagrant miscarriage of justice had taken place. They took action which resulted in the law eventually being changed and the principle of an accused being innocent until proved guilty confirmed in an amended Act of Parliament. (Shamefully, it took a further sixteen years – until 1911 – for this to happen during which time all of those unfortunates accused of certain offences had to somehow prove their innocence or they were judged guilty.)

Positive proof of prescriptive possession

The evidence inadvertently brought out in the unfair prosecution of the Tyson case emphatically proved that the river had been freely and legally fished by local anglers, specifically at the level of the Haining beat. There was also corroborated evidence that the Haining Estate had prescriptive possession during the crucially important period from 1870 to 1912.

This was the last handful of sand thrown into our eyes by the Crown's representatives and the last thing we had to prove in order to succeed.

But for the incompetence of a lawyer the adverse claim to the Crown Estate could have been settled much earlier, much time and effort could have been spared, and horrendously expensive legal costs incurred by the Crown could have been avoided. It was these lawyers' fees which ultimately proved the catalyst to the Crown Estate's capitulation and acceptance of our adverse claim. Our legal costs had been a few postage stamps.

For us it was a highly satisfying and justified outcome that had given us an insight into a fascinating episode of local history.

Our research revealed how the unfair treatment meted out to a habitual and many times convicted Selkirk poacher had changed the law of the land. It also showed to several of the SAA that some lawyers, sheriffs, crown officials and civil servants can be inefficient or untrustworthy at times and should be regarded with circumspection!

It was confirmed by Anne Chapman of Anderson Strathern representing the Crown Estate on 5 Feb 2016 that the Crown Estates were in the process of transmitting a signed disposition of the Haining salmon fishings in favour of the Haining Trust.

That was our 'VE' day - Victory Ettrick day!

Conclusion of the Recovery of the Haining Stretch

Overall conclusion of the war

During the prolonged campaign to restore to the various owners of fishing rights and to confirm what had been theirs and not the Crown's, we managed to establish certain things.

Far from being unchartered as the Crown representatives claimed, we had uncovered evidence that the Ettrick had been chartered uninterruptedly for at least 200 years. In every area that the Crown representatives maintained were unchartered and therefore theirs to freely acquire, we found there were charters. If they were accessible to us, they were equally accessible to the Crown's representatives. They had simply not bothered to look.

We had faced less than gentlemanly tactics, encountered deliberate falsehoods and by doggedly opposing every manoeuvre and wily tactic the Crown Estate emerged with, had caused them to incur huge legal bills.

Their relentless pursuit of what they claimed was theirs inspired us to demonstrate continuously that their case was untenable. We were only able to do this because of the quality of the legal advice we obtained from Sheriff Drummond.

If the Crown Estates' predecessors had fulfilled their undertaking to research the true ownership of the rights between 1912 and 1914 they could have averted their legal costs.

However, by contesting the chartered rights which had been partially conceded in 1912 by HMW, the Crown squandered a significant amount of money that would otherwise have enriched their coffers and helped to pay for the monarchy's upkeep.

We had retained for the Selkirk anglers their right to fish the Ettrick in Selkirk as of old and also the Estate Waters upstream as their forefathers had done. It had cost the anglers many thousands of pounds in leasing fees over the years which the Crown had wrongly pocketed. We had no desire to recover these wrongful payments to the Crown, even though it was stated that "the Crown Estates do not give back money". At least it will have gone some way towards settling their legal costs.

The outcomes achieved by us in 2006 and 2016 proved once and for all that the Crown Estates had no justification in claiming ownership of fishing rights in the Ettrick and charging rent to anglers to fish for virtually 100 years. New leases were negotiated by the SAA with the Philiphaugh Estate, the Haining Trust and the Selkirk Common Good Fund for about a tenth of what the CE was trying to charge.

The Crown Estate was right to surrender when it did for we had enough additional evidence at our disposal had we been forced to go to court. The SAA had been salting money away for years against the possibility of a court action so litigation held no fears for us. The Crown Estate would have ended up being publicly shamed.

So the anglers can be happy and have a song in their hearts as they stand and try to catch an Ettrick salmon!

By detailing the steps we had to take, the obduracy of the Crown Estates and at times their downright rudeness, we may be able provide others with hints on how to take on a large enterprise possessing many advantages compared to their own, and win. We did not just win, but checked them in every devious move the Crown Estates devised (and they devised many), before they finally capitulated and ended up checkmated. Their defeat was complete, very low key, little advertised, but utterly delightful! The CEC never did admit on paper that they had lost, they simply did some legal fiddling and went away.

Such was the injury to the pride of the Crown Estates that they did not officially communicate to the Selkirk Angling Association that they had conceded that the rights were owned by the Haining Estate. In order to confirm that the Crown Estates had withdrawn their claim of ownership we contacted the CEC's lawyers by telephone to have confirmed that indeed they had. We judged this pretty shameful and arrogant behaviour!

A Final Irony

The slump in Atlantic salmon catches in Scottish rivers affected the Tweed and its tributaries equally. Numbers being caught in the 21st century are a fraction of totals recorded even twenty years ago and, whereas fishing rights changed hands at substantial sums of money, the poor catches in recent years have devalued fishing properties.

The irresponsible destruction of Selkirk's Cauld with the consequent loss of the seven important fishing pools, climate change, and the uncontrolled trawling for salmon at sea have probably all contributed to what is now a negligible number of salmon caught in the Ettrick. Most fish are now returned as demanded by the regulations, owing to their scarcity.

A further irony is the outcome of immature farmed salmon escaping from cages in sea lochs on the Scottish West Coast. Being genetically similar, although quite distinct from the native salmon genotype when fully mature, there is a risk that these immigrants may eventually be able to interbreed with the local wild variety and result in genetic pollution. The danger of this is still to be evaluated, but in 2020 more than 25,000 escaped which vastly outnumbered the local salmon population.

So was the long battle worth it?

Certainly it was; the leasing charges are now realistic and the Angling Association has some say in setting the level. The fishing stocks will improve over time – perhaps it will take many years. The Haining Trust now benefits from an annual leasing fee for its property, the Philiphaugh Estate has its fishings back and Selkirk Burgh has regained the Town Water which it had for about 750 years – an asset taken from, and eventually returned to, the Selkirk Common Good Fund.

Over the years the Crown illegally gained about £25,000 in leasing charges which, in defiance of common law, they refused to pay back. At the same time, by their own admission, they incurred avoidable and eye-watering legal fees all to no purpose. Had their predecessors carried through their commitment to research the ownership in the pre WWI period, much expenditure could have been saved in the 21st century.

For the researchers the campaign was enormous fun and took us into historical nooks and crannies too numerous to be included in this account. The discovery of an original charter, stumbling in 2005 upon the forgotten correspondence from HMW 1910 - 1925, and bringing to light the story of the reprobate poacher who changed the law of the country – all were fantastic strokes of good fortune and irresistible inducements to carry on the campaign..

For the historians and fishermen of the Selkirk and District Angling Association it has been a fascinating insight into the behaviour of seemingly fair-minded national bodies and into corners of history which will never again be so thoroughly visited nor result in an ultimate outcome to take such delight in.

This was one big fish that didn't get away!

One question remains; how can a respected body such as the Crown Estate take something it didn't own, then give it back to its original owner as though it were an act of munificent generosity and profit from its seizure? Is that legal?

Acknowledgements

Various people gave their time and expertise at different stages in the campaign and they played crucial roles at times in underpinning our case. Future generations of Souters* have reason to be grateful to them as they all helped to restore to Selkirk, Philiphaugh, and the Haining what had always been their property but had been taken away from them.

In 1989 the late David Neate, a long time SAA member, started inquiries into fishing rights ownership. He deserves credit for starting the ball rolling in questioning the Crown's claims of ownership.

In 1992 Andrew Murray, former secretary of the SAA, passed on David Neate's notes to Dr Lindsay Neil and asked him (me) to continue to pursue the investigations. I took up the challenge. As a nearly retired Selkirk GP it was an offer I couldn't refuse and it became a pastime pursuit of continuing and unending interest.

David Mitchell, Secretary of the SAA, a keen fisherman himself, knew a great deal of 20th century history of local salmon fishing and of the Selkirk club. He contributed hugely.

Adam Borwick, Ex GPO administrator and successor to David Mitchell above, a keen and active SAA member and also a keen fisherman, was enormously helpful with his extensive knowledge of fishing.

Sheriff Kevin Drummond QC, Sheriff of Selkirk, now retired, gave invaluable legal advice continually and over a long period. His contribution was crucial in framing our discussions with the CEC in legally correct content, language and format. His lancing legal insight and experience was enormously helpful.

A Souter is a citizen born and brought up in Selkirk. It is an old Scots term for a maker of 'single-soled shoon' – shoes – and a soubriquet proudly owned in Selkirk-born folk by those who qualify.

Sir David Steel MP (subsequently Lord Steel of Aikwood) for his liaison with Crown Estates. His interventions and successful overcoming of local authority obfuscation, were signally helpful.

Alisdair Wilson, Treasurer of SAA and longtime member, was able to contribute the financial history of SAA from the club records.

James Handyside and Colin Cairney, both Presidents of SAA, gave their support and that of the Association which validated our researches. Without the club's support, the research and actions taken would not have been worthwhile.

All the above were members of the SAA. Both they and other members were able to volunteer reminiscences and information.

Sir Michael Strang Steel, owner of Philiphaugh Estate, provided Estate papers and support. His foresight in allying his Estate's cause with our own was a crucial advantage. Subsequently he agreed a nominal annual lease for Philiphaugh Water.

Graham Phillips, Sir Michael's lawyer of Morrisons WS of Glasgow, made some important contributions with regard to the Philiphaugh Estate's interests and, along with a colleague, uncovered the lost 1910-1925 correspondence. These finds in the Glasgow cellar verified all the painstaking records of Burgh clerks in the early 20th century.

The late Brian Gilmour, lawyer in Selkirk, gave us initial legal advice pro bono and, clarified the law pertaining to salmon fishing and the rights thereto. He gave us our first glimpse of the legal minefield we were getting into!

Teresa Maley identified the Philiphaugh Barony Charter and corrected a rough translation from the original Latin. Her facility in decoding complex ancient texts was fascinating to watch.

Alan Davidson, June Pringle and Ian Hope, great-grandchildren of Bat Tyson, who helped identify the photograph of Bat Tyson and lent others. Their contribution gave us the ammunition to destroy the crown's claims of ownership of the Haining stretch and overcome the last hurdle.

Bill Chisholm from Jedburgh helped with the manuscript. His experience as a journalist was useful in discouraging verbosity.

Ian Collie, an Ex Gordonstounian lawyer who witnessed signed affidavits demanded by the CE and did it pro bono at pretty short notice.

Janis Cornwall, a vastly experienced doyenne of the local press who lent some of her own painting and photography work.

Lyon and Turnbull, auctioneers, whose experts failed to recognise a Royal Charter granting a barony. Had the manuscript been correctly identified as an original Royal Charter, it would probably not have been bought on spec as barony charters command a much higher price than a simple land transfer deed, which is what it was thought to be.

Mrs Susan Edington, the Haining Trust's lawyer and chairperson, for permitting us to pursue the rights on behalf of the Haining Trust.

Staff of the Selkirk Weekend Advertiser and the Borders Telegraph for publishing the 1913 pictures which uncovered Bat Tyson.

The ordinary members of the SAA, which has been in existence since the middle 1800s, who contributed their support, some interesting memories and some background anecdotes.

Mrs Pat Neil who was able to reprise her assistant editorship with Macmillans Publishers and proofread her husband's mangled English.

James and Cath Rutherford, and Louise Scott of Bordersprint. Their experience in graphics and layout for printing was most helpful in pulling this book together.

APPENDICES

Appendix A

Copy of the original correspondence sent to the lawyers representing Philiphaugh Estate (part of the 'Glasgow Hoard'). A more peremptory letter was received by Selkirk Burgh Council requesting information, and it was only in 2005 that we discovered that the Crown Authorities in 1910 had known all along that Philiphaugh was a barony with ownership of fishings.

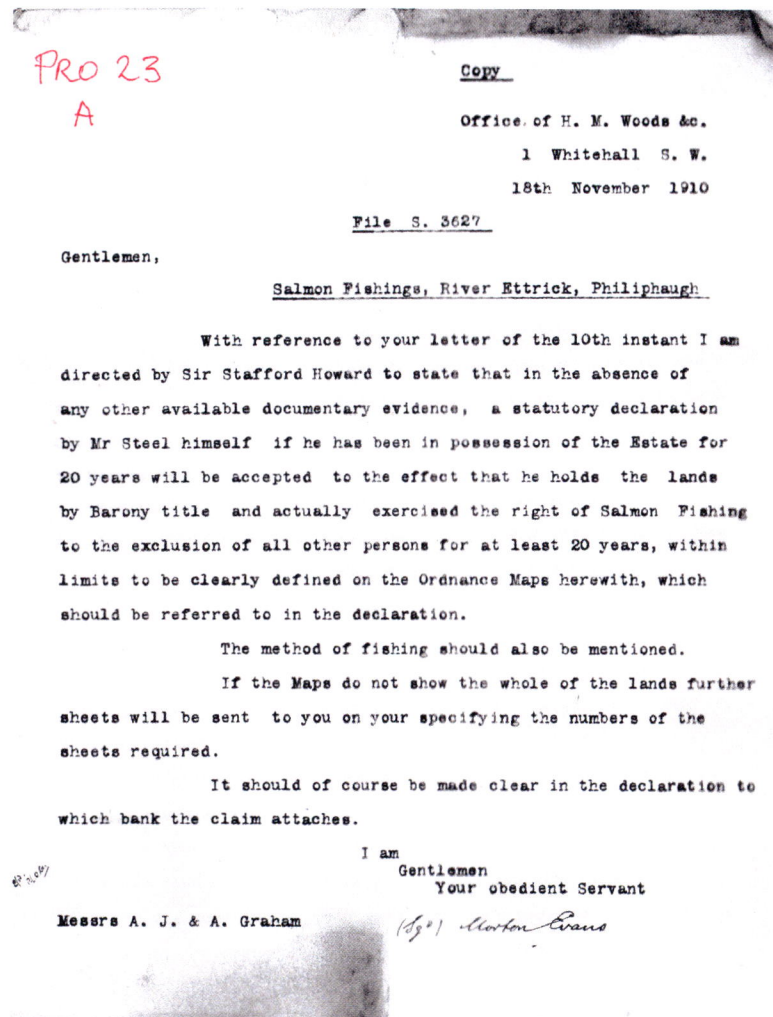

PRO 23
A

Copy

Office of H. M. Woods &c.
1 Whitehall S. W.
18th November 1910

File S. 3627

Gentlemen,

Salmon Fishings, River Ettrick, Philiphaugh

With reference to your letter of the 10th instant I am directed by Sir Stafford Howard to state that in the absence of any other available documentary evidence, a statutory declaration by Mr Steel himself if he has been in possession of the Estate for 20 years will be accepted to the effect that he holds the lands by Barony title and actually exercised the right of Salmon Fishing to the exclusion of all other persons for at least 20 years, within limits to be clearly defined on the Ordnance Maps herewith, which should be referred to in the declaration.

The method of fishing should also be mentioned.

If the Maps do not show the whole of the lands further sheets will be sent to you on your specifying the numbers of the sheets required.

It should of course be made clear in the declaration to which bank the claim attaches.

I am
Gentlemen
Your obedient Servant

Messrs A. J. & A. Graham   (Sgd) Morton Evans

165

Appendix B

Two public notices, one from 1817, the other from 1806, reinforcing fishing laws, in particular the ban on Sunday fishing.

Each notice confirms that it was a Burgh task to control fishing, hinting that the Burgh therefore had prescriptive possession. It is not specific to the Ettrick and therefore not submitted to the Crown Estate as evidence.

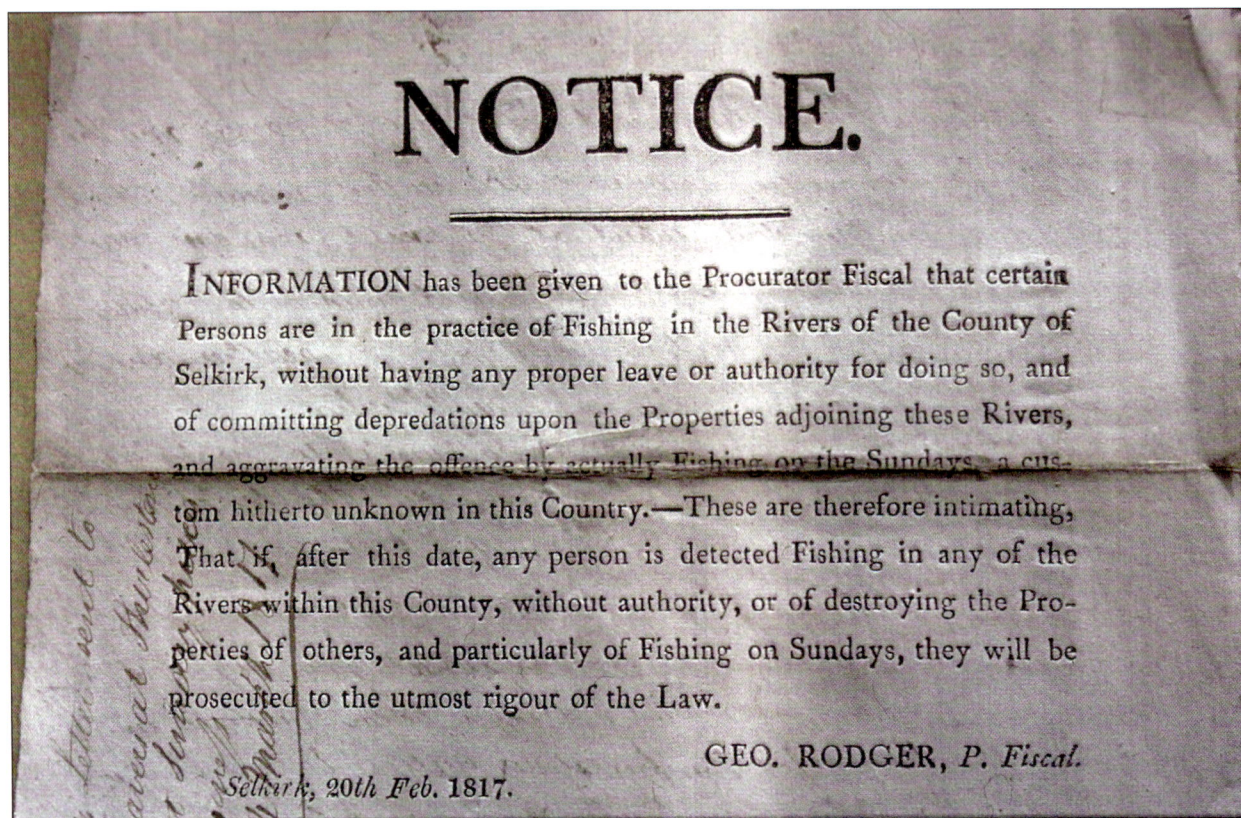

NOTICE.

INFORMATION has been given to the Procurator Fiscal that certain Persons are in the practice of Fishing in the Rivers of the County of Selkirk, without having any proper leave or authority for doing so, and of committing depredations upon the Properties adjoining these Rivers, and aggravating the offence by actually Fishing on the Sundays, a custom hitherto unknown in this Country.—These are therefore intimating, That if, after this date, any person is detected Fishing in any of the Rivers within this County, without authority, or of destroying the Properties of others, and particularly of Fishing on Sundays, they will be prosecuted to the utmost rigour of the Law.

GEO. RODGER, *P. Fiscal.*

Selkirk, 20*th Feb.* 1817.

1817 Notice

Notice to the Public.

THE Procurator Fiscal in the County of Selkirk, being specially instructed to use every legal measure to prevent Fishing in Close-time, and to co-operate with others as much as lies in his power for that purpose, confiders it proper to lay before the Public a brief Abstract of the Laws regarding the Fisheries of the Tweed, and the Streams communicating with the same; in order that no person may plead ignorance thereof, if found guilty in contravening the same.

Fishing Laws before referred to.

By Statute 11th George III. Cap. 37, amended by Statute 15th George III. the following Enactments are made regarding the Fisheries in the River Tweed and Streams running into the same.

1st. Persons killing Salmon, Gilse, Salmon-Trout, or Whitling, between the 10th of October and the 10th of January, or between ten o'clock on Saturday night and two o'clock on Monday morning, shall forfeit any Sum not exceeding Ten Pounds, nor less than Forty Shillings, for every such Fish.

2d. Persons killing, or having in their possession, any spawn, Fry, or Young Brood of any of the said Fish, between the 1st day of April and the 1st day of June, shall forfeit and pay the sum of Ten Shillings for every parcel thereof.

3d. Persons beating the water, putting up any white object, or in any other manner preventing the Fish entering the River Tweed, or the Streams, &c. communicating with it, shall for every offence forfeit and pay any sum not exceeding Five Pounds, nor less than Ten Shillings Sterling.

4th. Any Person laying Lint, Dirt, Rubbish, &c. in the River or Streams, to forfeit Twenty Shillings Sterling.

5th. Prosecutions are appointed to be brought before any one or more of the Justices of the Peace or the Sheriff of the County wherein the Offender resides. The proof requisite to establish guilt, is the confession of the Party accused, or the testimony of one or more credible witness or witnesses; and the mode of enforcing payment of the penalty is, by distress, and Sale of the Offender's Goods and Chattels; and if the penalties are not forthwith paid and satisfied, the Judge is authorised to commit the Offender to the common jail, or house of correction, for any time not exceeding three months, nor less than one month.

The Procurator Fiscal also takes this opportunity of representing to the Public, that he is informed the practice of shooting House Pigeons is become so prevalent and common, that he will be under the necessity of instituting prosecutions against such persons as may be guilty thereof, in order to put a stop to such improper and unwarrantable conduct in time coming. And with respect to Poaching, the Procurator Fiscal expects that more attention will be paid to the Game Laws than has hitherto been done, otherwise those found guilty of contravening the same, after this public caution, may rest assured that they will be proceeded against with the utmost rigour, and for which they will have themselves only to blame.

Moreover, it may not be improper to observe, that persons so conducting themselves are liable to be prosecuted by the Proprietor of the grounds upon which they may trespass, for damages done thereto, and for breaking down and destroying the Fences thereof.

GEORGE RODGER, P. F.

Selkirk, 5th Aug. 1806.

Printed by Robert Armstrong, Hawick.

1806 Notice saying much the same. It simply confirms that there was judicial supervision of the fishing in the local tributaries of the Tweed. It did not really help our case.

167

Appendix C

Summary of Burgh Council Minutes 1910-1914

Selkirk Burgh Council hunts for evidence of ownership but finally agrees to the lease.

<u>SUMMARY OF RELEVANT ENTRIES IN SELKIRK BURGH COUNCIL MINUTES 1910-1914</u>

31.1.1910   In response to a general enquiry into fishing rights by the Crown Receiver, the Burgh Clerk goes to Edinburgh and states to the Crown Receiver that under "present or former charters, the Burgh has right to the salmon fishings".

The Council approves action of the Burgh Clerk.

14.11.1910   Reported that HM Woods in a letter asks for description of fishings claimed and disputes that there is a grant of fishings.

The Burgh Clerk is instructed to investigate and report back.

6.3.1911   The Burgh Clerk reports that he had been unable to discover any charter or record of rights to fishing. He states that there was local belief that the fishings were let (by the Burgh) in approx 1850.

Clerk asked to research accounts for that period and report back.

3.4.1911   Clerk reports letter received from HM Woods dated 18.3.1911 rejecting Burgh's claim to title as Burgh has neither "express grant or Habile Title" but accepts that the Burgh's view could differ.

1.5.1911   Burgh Clerk reports that local historian T. Craig Brown had researched charters and valuation rolls at passing of Valuation Act, which revealed no express grant of fishings. But he says Burgh may have right as successor to Douglas family to "fisheries belonging to the lands, lordship and barony of Selkirk".

5.6.1911   Burgh Clerk reports letter from HM Woods that HM Woods doubts that Selkirk has Habile Title but accepts that "exclusive possession" following a Habile Title would displace the Crown's rights. HM Woods would not accept that earlier references to "fishings" referred to salmon fishings. Also enquires how the fishings have been dealt with during (say) the last twenty years.

Clerk to reply to HM Woods.

4.9.1911   Clerk reports letter from HM Woods, July 1911. HM Woods can see "no sufficient ground for admitting a claim by the Burgh to salmon fishing". Accordingly pronounces them "unchartered" and claims them for the Crown.

4.3.1912   Despite letter dated July 1911 claiming Crown's rights to fishings in Ettrick, new letter dated 16.2.1912 admits "Investigation of titles in this river is not yet complete"... "as a temporary measure pending a decision as to future dealing with fishings found to belong to the Crown, to allow the Town Council to exercise the Crown's rights . . . ex adverso of their lands . . on payment of a small acknowledgement for the season". HM Woods offers to submit a model of system of fishings as used in Ayr.

Council defers decision.

1.4.1912   Specimen of Crown's let of fishings to Burgh of Ayr
considered. Council decides conditions therein were "totally
inapplicable" to the Ettrick. Resolved to advise HM Woods of this
opinion but in order "to retain for the benefit of the public,
the rights now claimed by the Crown, and until such time as the
Crown has completed its investigation of titles . . . to offer as
an acknowledgement of said rights a sum of 2/6d."

Clerk asked to write to HM Woods.

6.5.1912   In a letter, HM Woods proposes to grant a lease for
1 year for £1/=/= provided "charges to the public are only nominal".
The Council agrees to pay £1/=/= in respect of "rights now claimed
by the Crown" for fishings and formulate regulations.

3.6.1912   Council agrees that the fishing regulations drawn up
by the Town Clerk should be submitted to HM Woods.

Early July 1912 Council receives letter from HM Woods of 27.6.1912
approving town's regulations, stating inter alia that "the arrangement
is to be temporary and experimental only, until it is seen how it
works and whether any other fishings may be included, the consideration
of the question of a formal lease being in the meantime deferred".
The Council agrees to approve the terms and conditions, "it being
understood, as therein stated, that the arrangement is to be only
temporary and experimental", and "as the Crown's exclusive rights
extend only to salmon, seatrout and fish of the salmon kind", i.e.
excluding trout etc which are not included in the regulations.

22.7.1912   HM Woods in a letter dated 13.7.1912 states that the
Twon Council for 1 year "are now at liberty to proceed with issue of
permits".

3.2.1913   Letter from HM Woods dated 1.2.1913 offering a further
stretch of fishings, asking what "the Council consider would be a
fair rent for (1) the salmon fishings in the waters that were let to
them last season, and (2) for the additional waters". The Council
instruct the Clerk to reply "that it was distinctly understood when
the terms of the let were being discussed last year that the rent was
to be nominal and that the charge for permits was fixed accordingly,
that the rent of £1 payable last season should not be disturbed, or
that if it is to be increased at all it should be to a very slight
extent and certainly not to exceed £2 per annum". The Clerk was also
invited to enquire to whom the further stretches of fishing might be
let if the town did not take up HM Woods' offer.

13.3.1913   A letter was read confirming the let of fishings for
a further year. The further fishings are mentioned in the letter as
being held over for further consideration.

6.4.1914   HM Woods has offered a 10-year lease at £5/=/= p.a.
Council agrees terms of the lease except the rent and decides to
offer £3/=/=.

7.9.1914   Council approves an amended 10-year lease at £5/=/= p.a.
Subsequent entries refer mainly to people fishing illegally and being
banned.

Appendix D

The sequence of the Barony of Selkirk title transfers mainly to the Douglas Family. In 1747, the barony privileges became owned by Selkirk Burgh under an Act of the Parliament of Great Britain.

Burgh Status of Selkirk and when it was a Barony

The question is, when did Selkirk Burgh inherit the privileges and titles of the Barony of Selkirk, conferred frequently and most recently on the Douglas family (Earls of Angus)?

Barony titles carrying fishing rights were usually specified.

Unless granted separately, it is always assumed a barony title carried the right to fish for salmon where relevant. In the case of Selkirk, fishing was specified in several barony charters including those of 1565 and 1602. Selkirk was also confirmed as a barony in 1668 in an unrelated dispute in the Court of Session between the Laird of Haining and Selkirk Burgh.

History

Selkirk was granted as a barony on numerous occasions and originally mentioned in grants of charters to support the abbey (built 1109-1113). Subsequently, the Douglas family were granted the barony by the Scottish monarch, but periodically lost it through changing allegiance to the English side:

1109   Abbey / Monastery in Tyron founded, Radulfus sent to Selkirk to be abbot of Selkirk. (Liber de Mailros) NAS and SBC archives.

By **1113**, Earl David, 6th son of Malcolm III, was granted most of Southern Scotland by his brother, Alexander I.

1119   Charter of foundation Selkirk Abbey. Specifies land and fishings. (Copied into Liber de Calchou c. 1320) NAS

1130s King David I declares Ettrick Forest a Royal Demesne. These had an area of common land within them.

1147 Charter of Removal of abbey to Kelso. Identical grant of fishings. (Liber de Calchou)

1159 King Malcolm IV (grandson of David 1) grants fishing rights of "my waters around Selkirk" to the monks of Kelso in common with "my people of Selkirk". Identical with 1119 and 1147 charters. (NAS, Advocates Lib.)

In **1306** Edward I grants the barony of Selkirk to Aymer de Valence, an English knight, later Lord Pembroke. Bannockburn terminates the arrangement.

1314 The barony may have been granted to Sir James Douglas following Bannockburn.

Selkirk is acknowledged as a Burgh by 1328

1321-22 Selkirk, Ettrick and Traquair forests definitely granted to Sir James Douglas as a free barony, confirmed in 1324.

1335 Edward II grants town and shire of Selkirk, Ettrick forest and Selkirk forest to William de Montecute.

1354 David II confirms William , Lord Douglas of Liddesdale in the above after first being named in 1345.

1366 The 'lands of Selkirk' were granted to Robert Dalzell. This is anomalous.

1384 The barony goes to Liddesdale's son James who was killed at the battle of Otterburn in 1388. He claimed it from William, 1st Earl of Douglas who, having succeeded from his uncle Hugh, died intestate in 1384.

1398 Granted to George Douglas, Earl of Angus.

1401 After Hamildon Hill, Henry IV grants "Lordship of Selkirk, Ettrick, Ettrick forest and everything that to the forest pertains" to Henry Percy, Earl of Northumberland.

1411 James I, a prisoner in England grants the lands of Drumlanrig, Hawick & Selkirk to his cousin, William Douglas of Drumlanrig (the Red Douglas of Angus).

1451 James II reaffirms the 1449 Act of Parliament and Royal Charter giving William, Earl of Douglas, "forestlands of Ettrick & Selkirk" **including fishing**. (CB, II, p.94; Act of Parliament 1449, ii, 63; Book of the Great Seal, ?1449, ii, 308)

1455 James II annexes all the lands to the crown and everything granted to the Douglases (originally by Robert the Bruce in 1314).

1488 Lordship of Selkirkshire restored to Earl of Angus by James IV.

1489 Angus forfeits his lands to James IV but gets them back.

1498 Inherited by George Douglas, heir to Archibald Douglas, Earl of Angus.

[Throughout these ownerships, it remained a Royal Burgh and a free barony, not a Burgh of Barony.]

1511 James IV grants lands at Elibank but expressly excludes "the fishing of salmon, le kipper and smoltis" (CB p.131).

1532 Angus sides with Henry of England and loses his lands.

1535 (actually **4th Mar. 1536**) James V re-grants burgh status to Selkirk. Includes Burgh rights.

1543 James V gives the lands back to Angus after James IV had died.

1567 Mary Queen of Scots ratifies the Earldom of Angus to Archibald Douglas and amongst the many titles confirmed, is the barony of Selkirk, **including the fishings (piscariis).** Acta Parliamentorum Mariae, **1567**, No 20 – **have copy.**

1585 Angus gets back his lands which he had lost again.

1602 (1603) James VI confirms the barony title of Selkirk **"cum...piscariis"** to William Douglas, Earl of Angus, as a "Free Burgh of Barony" – "in liberos burgos baronie" (plural, along with others).

[Selkirk Burgh administered the Angus lands and privileges, the barony being a 'burgh of barony' but in fact with the Earl of Angus only collected the income, taking little part in the administration.]

1668 Riddell of Haining contests the Burgh's commons rights and loses at the Court of Session. Court confirms that **the common is part of a barony**. Haining is censured for causing riots. His animals are allowed to graze the Common.

1681 An act of Parliament giving away substantial portions of Selkirk's Common is passed, **confirming Selkirk's entitlement to the remainder**. Fishing is not mentioned.

1707 Union of Parliaments, the status of Burghs of Barony questionable.

1744 The Duke of Douglas, heritor of the barony, tries to impose his choice of magistrate on the town, but loses after Selkirk appeals to the House of Lords.

1747 (1748) Act of George II abolishing hereditary entitlement to appoint sheriffs and to have jurisdiction over people in their baronies, sheriffdoms etc, but this right was to remain with Royal Burghs. The act somewhat obliquely abolishes burghs of barony. Barony rights regarding land and other privileges are specifically retained by barons, baronies and Burghs.

1748 The Duke of Douglas claims £34,000 for loss of regality of his burgh of barony, including £2,000 for Selkirk; he gets given £5,100 and goes away. **Neither he nor his successors play any subsequent part in any Selkirk affairs**.

1795 Act of George III re-establishing burghs of barony **referring to their abolition in 1747 by George II**, but only in respect of Scottish coastal towns to promote the fishing industry.

After **1747** Selkirk Town Council administered unmolested the barony lands and privileges, **including fishings**, until the Crown contested the fishing rights in 1910. We have documentary evidence for this.

At the very least, Selkirk can claim prescriptive possession of the fishing from 1748 until 1910.

The barony entitlements legally passed to Selkirk Town Council in 1748. They were certainly in Selkirk's possession by 1785.

Compiled from T Craig Brown's 'History of Selkirkshire' 1886
and 'The Douglas Book', 1886 by Sir William Fraser, III, 36; NLS

Appendix. E
Letter from Sir David Steel to Chairman CEC

Aikwood Tower

Selkirk   10 November 2003

<u>Fishings in Selkirk currently leased from the Crown by Selkirk Angling Association.</u>

Dear Ian,

The lease to Selkirk of the fishings on the Ettrick has continued in an uninterrupted fashion since the Crown laid claim to the rights in 1910. Prior to that, Selkirk believed it had the rights to fish under ancient grants of title to Common Lands bordering the river, and did so. The outbreak of WW1 foreshortened the continuing negotiations, but it was mutually agreed that the rental would be 'nominal', that the Crown would investigate the relevant titles and that the arrangement entered into would be 'experimental and temporary'. The original lease was for £5 per annum.

Selkirk never accepted the Crown's rights claimed between 1910 and 1914, but acknowledged their claim.

The recent rapid increase in the leasing charge, which is now £4,000 per annum, has landed the Angling Association with a difficult situation. Some of their members are OAPs and cannot afford the necessary cost of a permit, which will now be £100+ per annum.

In view of there being no record of the Crown investigating the various titles, some members did their own research and have uncovered some interesting facts.

The Crown has been leasing fishing rights to Selkirk, half of which is actually owned by Philiphaugh Estates. A charter from James VI is incontrovertible evidence for this and the original charter is in private hands in Selkirk.

Extensive research into historical documents and archives relating to the other part of the river that abuts on Selkirk Burgh land, has been undertaken. The research strongly supports that the fishing rights are indeed part of Selkirk's common inheritance. The charters have not survived but their existence, and the rights to fish that they contained, is verified in later and related Royal charters. There is also ample evidence that salmon fishing was carried out without hindrance by the Burghers for at least 100 years before the Crown made its claim.

The Angling Association do not wish to become involved in costly legal wrangling and have been very reluctant to pursue their claim, but are now persuaded that to secure fishing for their older members and for the future, they will have to assert Selkirk's right. They do not wish to seek redress for charges erroneously levied by the Crown in the past.

It struck me that the matter could be agreed and settled without recourse to a necessarily public airing of the issues involved and I obtained their assent to approach you.

They propose to enter into a leasing arrangement with Philiphaugh Estates for the rights to their part of the river and wish the Crown to recognise the Burgh's rights to the remainder currently leased from the Crown.

Yours etc.
David Steel

This was the letter that produced a response from the Crown Estates suggesting the submission of an adverse claim.

Appendix F

Blank adverse claim form; what we were required to submit

NOTES FOR THE GUIDANCE OF CLAIMANTS TO SALMON FISHINGS

The right to fish for salmon is _prima facie_ vested in the Sovereign and anyone claiming to possess such right over any stretch of sea, river or inland water should produce for consideration evidence of,

(1)   a direct grant from the Crown specifically of the right to salmon fishing over the stretch of water in question or

(2)   a Barony title coupled with clear and unequivocal possession of the salmon fishings for a prescriptive period which is still twenty years or

(3)   a direct grant from the Crown of the general right of fishings over the stretch of water in question coupled with clear and unequivocal possession of the salmon fishings for the prescriptive period.

(4)   By concession the Crown Estate is also prepared to admit claims based on:-

a)   a title from a subject specifically conveying the right to salmon fishing over the stretch of water in question coupled with possession of the salmon fishings for twenty years; or

(b)   a title from a subject conveying a general right of fishings over the stretch of water in question coupled with clear and unequivocal possession of the salmon fishings for the twenty year prescriptive period.

In the evidence produced by the claimant is sufficient in the opinion of the Commissioners as then advised to establish that the Crown has been divested of its ownership of the salmon fishings the claim may be admitted by them in respect of the Crown's interest, but in that respect only, without further formality. It is stressed that if the matter is to be dealt with on this informal basis the evidence must be such as might reasonably be thought would produce the same conclusion should the matter be tested in Court.

The enclosed claim form has been framed to give a general indication of the matters requiring to be proved by the Claimant to facilitate enquiries but nothing in these notes or claim form precludes the Commissioners from requiring further information and evidence.

It is suggested that if the claimant can co-operate by producing all the necessary evidence when submitting his claim so that the claim can by taken without prolonged delays and correspondence.

CLAIM TO SALMON FISHINGS, SCOTLAND

NAME OF CLAIMANT:

ADDRESS

ESTATE OR PROPERTY OWNED BY CLAIMANT:

LOCATION OF SALMON FISHINGS CLAIMED:

NAME AND ADDRESS OF AGENTS:

TO BE COMPLETED IN ALL CASES

1. The claim is based on:

Delete as
Appropriate

(a) a Crown Charter specifically conveying salmon fishings.

(b) a Barony title linked with clear and unequivocal possession of the salmon fishings for the prescriptive period.

(c) a Crown Charter conveying fishings linked with clear and unequivocal possession of the salmon fishings for the prescriptive period.

(d) a title from a subject conveying specifically the right to salmon fishing over the stretch of water in question coupled with possession of the salmon fishings for the prescriptive period; or

(e) a title from a subject conveying a general right of fishings over the stretch of water in question coupled with clear and unequivocal possession of the salmon fishings for the prescriptive period.

2. The stretch of salmon fishings to which this claim relates is delineated and coloured   on the Ordnance Survey map annexed and signed as relative hereto.

177

In addition, further questions were to be answered:

3. The writ founded on is: -
   which, or a certified copy of which, with a translation if in Latin, is produced

4. The date of the claimants title if not specified above, which is produced

5. The description of the said writ (No. 3 above) is as follows:-

6. Description of claimant's title if different

7. Acts of Possession

8. Exhibition of catch returns

Thus we were obliged to submit our claim in this very strict format.

Appendix G

Supportive evidence for Selkirk's case

Barony of Selkirk confirmation: case in the Court of Session

(Corroboration of the sequence of Baronies granted to the Douglas Family) *Appendix D*

In 1668 The Laird of Haining claimed entitlement to pasturage on Selkirk Common in an action in the Court of Session. The Burgh had tried to deny him access for his animals on the grounds that he did not have grazing rights. The Burgh lost and Haining won but the action inter alia (among other things) emphatically confirmed that Selkirk was indeed a barony with concomitant barony rights. However, because the Haining owner's case was not about fishing rights we were advised it could not be used in support of Selkirk's claim to the fishing because it was not an original foundation writ. This finding was separate from the barony of Selkirk granted to the Douglas family which did specify fishing and was a foundation writ.

(Taken from Craig Brown 'History of Selkirkshire' 1886)

Appendix H

Letter of rejection from the Crown Estates 2004

Alan S Menzies W.S.
1 Rutland Court
Edinburgh
EH3 8EY

Crown Estate Solicitor (Scotland)

Tel: +44 (0)131 2707700
Fax:+44 (0)131 2707788
DX EDS Edinburgh 1
E-mail: alan.menzies@andersonstrathern.co.uk

Dr Lindsay D Neil MB Chb DA
Woodlands
Selkirk   TD7 4ND

Our ref: DTS/ASM/CEC5000.65/a

Your ref: Date: 7 December 2004

Dear Sir

Adverse Claim to Salmon Fishings River Ettrick, Selkirk

I refer to previous correspondence in connection with the above and write to advise that I now have my principals' instructions having considered the position fully both in respect of the claim by Philiphaugh Estate and Selkirk Angling Club/the Burgh of Selkirk. I write to advise that neither claim fulfils the criteria necessary for a claim to be successful and therefore both claims are rejected.

With regard to the Philiphaugh Estate claim, although there appears to be a *habile* title there has been exclusive possession of the salmon fishing rights by the Crown Estate since at least the end of the First World War and no evidence of exclusive possession by the owners of Philiphaugh Estate has been presented.

As far as the other claim is concerned the Selkirk Angling Association as such would not appear to have any right to submit a claim as there does not appear to be any direct link between Scottish Borders Council as successors to Selkirk Burgh Council and their predecessors. If you propose to take the matter any further, before proceeding, a link would have to be demonstrated and some evidence that the pursuit of the claim is approved by Scottish Borders Council.

Turning to the evidence of possession of the fishings, the same comment applies that the Crown Estate has had exclusive possession of the salmon fishings since at least the end of the First World War.

For a claim to be successful it is necessary that a habile title is demonstrated and also that there has been exclusive possession of the salmon fishings for the prescriptive period which is now 20 years but prior to 1924 is 40 years.

Yours faithfully,

Alan S Menzies

Appendix I

Correspondence between CEC and SAA after the CEC's rebuttal letter *(Appendix H)* culminating in the hurriedly called meeting of 10 Jan 2006

AS
ANDERSON STRATHERN
SOLICITORS

Alan S Menzies W.S.
Crown Estate Solicitor (Scotland)

1 Rutland Court
Edinburgh
EH3 8EY
Tel: +44 (0)131 270 7700

David L Mitchell
Secretary
Selkirk & District Angling
Association
28 Scotts Place
SELKIRK
TD7 4DR

If calling please ask for | Diana Thurston Smith
Direct Dial | 0131 625 7231 | Fax: +44 (0)131 270 7788
Fax | 0131 625 8030 | DX: ED3 Edinburgh 1
Email | diana.thurstonsmith@ | E-mail: alan.menzies@
andersonstrathern.co.uk | andersonstrathern.co.uk

Our Ref: ASM/DTS/CEC5000.65/HDG

Your Ref:

Date: 4 November 2005

Dear Mr Mitchell

Adverse Claim to Salmon Fishings
River Ettrick - Selkirk

Thank you for your letter of 21 October 2005 addressed to my firm. I note all that you write and confirm that I now have instructions from my principals that a further meeting may be arranged for the end of November/beginning of December. The representatives on the Crown Estate side would include Sir Robert Clerk who manages the Crown Estate salmon fishings. The meeting could be held in my firm's offices but if that would be inconvenient for you please suggest an alternative venue. I look forward to hearing from you with suggested dates in due course.

As the Angling Association claim proceeds on different evidence to that produced in respect of Philiphaugh Estate, I am arranging a separate meeting with Sir Michael Strang Steel and his legal adviser.

Yours sincerely

Alan S Menzies

cc   Sir Robert Clerk Bt

INVESTOR IN PEOPLE

182

Smiths Gore • 12 Bernard Street • Edinburgh EH6 6PY • United Kingdom
t 0131 555 1200 • f 0131 554 2211 • dx 550854 Leith• www.smithsgore.co.uk

10 January 2006

D L Mitchell
Secretary, Selkirk and District Angling Association
Meadow Cottage
28 Scotts Place
SELKIRK
TD7 4DR

S
SMITHS

Our Ref   RMC/CRF/87-2
Your Ref

Dear David

The Crown Estate – Salmon Fishings
River Ettrick - Selkirk Burgh

Thank you for meeting me this morning, I found the friendly and constructive discussion with you and your colleagues most helpful. As promised I now write to confirm the proposals that I put forward on behalf of the Crown Estate which I hope will bring to an end the long debate about ownership of the River Ettrick salmon fishings at Selkirk. As I explained the Crown Estate is still of the view that the Selkirk Common Good Fund does not have a habile title to the claimed fishing interests but, with a view to bringing matters to a conclusion and to draw a line under past disagreement, the following solution is offered:-

1   The Crown Estate will sell to the Selkirk Common Good Fund (or to another suitable body should that be preferred) the right of salmon fishing in the River Ettrick at Selkirk, the extent of which is indicated in pink on the plan attached hereto. A price of £2,500 plus VAT will be paid to the Crown Estate for these rights and each party will bear their own professional costs.

2   Selkirk and District Angling Association will now relinquish the existing lease of salmon fishings at Selkirk dated 7 and 22 April 2003 held from the Crown Estate and will enter into a new lease from the Crown Estate of the 'Haynings' fishings, the extent of which is indicated in green of the plan attached hereto. This new lease will be for a term of 5 years from 1 January 2006 at an annual rent of £2,000 plus VAT and will otherwise be upon similar terms to the lease presently held by the Association.

Belford • Carlisle • Corbridge • Darlington • Dumfries • Edinburgh • Fochabers • Lichfield • Lincoln
London • Newmarket • Peterborough • Petworth • Preston • Winchester • Wrexham • York
Associated companies in British Virgin Islands • Denver • Kuala Lumpur • Sabah • Brunei

A list of partners is available from 17-18 Old Bond Street • London W1S 4PT • United Kingdom
Authorised and regulated by the Financial Services Authority. A member of primelocation.com

3   There will be no reimbursement of past rental payments received for these fishings by the Crown Estate.

As I explained to you this morning, prior to our meeting and acting on behalf of the Crown Estate I met with Sir Michael Strang Steel and made their offer to him namely that they will confirm that they have no further interest in the fishings claimed as part of Philiphaugh Estate on the understanding that in this case also that no claim will be made for past rents received by the Crown Estate in terms of previous leases of these fishings. I am hopeful that Sir Michael will agree to these terms and I understand that it would be his intention to grant a lease of the Philiphaugh salmon fishings on the Ettrick in favour of your association.

I very much hope that the terms of the Crown Estate's offer to your association as set out in this letter will be acceptable to your committee and to your membership. I think we are all agreed that these pragmatic proposals represent a better way forward for all concerned as an alternative to continuing and expensive legal debate and I look forward to hearing from you once you have been able to consult the Association's members at the forthcoming annual meeting.

Yours sincerely

Sir Robert M Clerk Bt. OBE FRICS
Consultant
e robert.clerk@smithsgore.co.uk • t Direct: 01968 677443

Offer from CEC, rejected by the SAA

Appendix J

2006. Letter from Sir Michael Strang Steel advising that any past rents recoverable were due to the SAA not Philiphaugh.

PHILIPHAUGH ESTATE OFFICE
PHILIPHAUGH
SELKIRK
TD7 5LX

Tel. & Fax: Selkirk (01750) 21766
Mobile: 07971 217459

Sir Robert Clerk Bt OBE FRICS
Consultant
Smiths Gore
12 Bernard Street
Edinburgh
EH6 6PY

17 January 2006

Your reference: RMC/CRF/87-2
Our ref: MSS/P16

PHILIPHAUGH ESTATE: THE PHILIPHAUGH TRUSTEES
THE CROWN ESTATE
SALMON FISHINGS: RIVER ETTRICK – SELKIRK

Thank you so much for your letter of 10 January following our meeting. I certainly agree that it would be good to have the matter of the Salmon Fishing interests settled.

You have proposed a pragmatic solution, whereby, insofar as the Philiphaugh stretch of the Ettrick (and the burn) is concerned, the Crown Estate will acknowledge that they have no continuing interest in these fishings. This will enable Philiphaugh Estate to exercise fishing rights or let the Salmon Fishings as they think fit. I assume – but perhaps you will confirm – that the acknowledgement will be for all time coming, so that the position is clear for the future and there will be no need to have further discussion or negotiation over the matter. Whether or not the Philiphaugh Trustees should seek some sort of conveyance I will leave to the lawyers, but it would be very helpful, I feel.

As I understand it, we have established Philiphaugh Estate's rights to the salmon fishing. If this is to apply for the future, it should, logically, also apply to the past and it would therefore follow that the Crown Estate have collected over many years rent to which they were not entitled. As I said to you, it was not my intention to reclaim on behalf of the Estate past rent paid by the Selkirk Angling Association. However, given that the iniative for clarifying the position of the Ettrick Salmon Fishings, has been taken by the Angling Association, who have after all paid the rent, I feel I should recommend to the Philiphaugh Trustees that their rights to claim past rents should be assigned to the Selkirk Angling Association.

This should allow the matter of the past rents to be discussed fully between the payers and the payees.

I hope we can now proceed on this basis and conclude this long running saga.

_WS._

Sir F M Strang Steel Bt CBE

Copy to: Dr L. Neil. Please show kevin too!

Michael

Due to the Angling Association, not Philiphaugh Estate.

185

Appendix K

Copy.

Sir E. Stafford Howard K.C.B.
H.M. Office of Woods &c.

1 Whitehall
LONDON   S.W.

OFFICE OF WOODS &c.

1, Whitehall, S.W.

198 West George Street,
GLASGOW, 28th March 1912.

Sir,

No. S 1188 - File S 3627
Salmon Fishings River Ettrick &c. Co. Selkirk
Philiphaugh

Gentlemen,

We have yours of yesterday.

We are obliged to you for the explanations and further information which you give us.   Provided it is clearly understood that our
Client's claim to the fishings is not prejudiced, we think he would be
disposed to concur in such a proposal as you suggest for a temporary
arrangement being made with the Town Council, as an experiment, subject
to revision hereafter if necessary.   Before submitting the suggestion
to him, however, we should like to have an outline of the scheme of
arrangement proposed, including the regulations under which it is
suggested the Town Council should issue permits.   If you can let us
have these, we shall put them before our Client, and ascertain whether
he acquiesces, and, if so, what further conditions, if any, he desires
have laid down with a view to the preservation of the amenity of his
property.

We are, Sir,

Your obedient Servants,

(Sgd.)   A. J. & A. GRAHAM.

Letter from Philiphaugh's lawyer to HMW asserting the Estate's claim in 1912. They never surrendered ownership.

186

Letter from William Strang Steel to Mr John Brown

Further proof of prescriptive possession by Philiphaugh Estate between 1888 and 1910.

It shows they fished their waters but actually outside the area leased to the SAA (the bit on the end that HMW had overlooked but which annulled their claim of ownership).

(Kindly found and lent by the late Douglas Scott of Heatherlie Antiques)

187

Appendix L

The final letter of capitulation.

Smiths Gore • 12 Bernard Street • Edinburgh EH6 6PY • United Kingdom
t 0131 555 1200 • f 0131 554 2211 • dx 550854 Leith• www.smithsgore.co.uk

30 January 2006

Dr Lindsay Neil MB ChB DA
Woodlands
Selkirk
TD7 4ND

SMITHSGORE

Our Ref   RMC/CR/CRF/87-2
Your Ref

Dear Dr Neil

The Crown Estate - Salmon Fishings
River Ettrick – Selkirk

Following our meeting on Friday afternoon I write to confirm the agreement we reached concerning the salmon fishing interests in the River Ettrick at Selkirk. I summarise the position as follows; -

1. Selkirk and District Angling Association will, with effect from 31st December 2005, relinquish the lease of salmon fishing interests at Selkirk held from the Crown Estate.

2. The Crown Estate will convey to the Selkirk Common Good Fund such salmon fishing interests as they may have in the river Ettrick at Selkirk which have been the subject of your claim. No consideration will be sought for these fishing interests and each party will bear their own expenses in the matter.

3. The Crown Estate will grant in favour of the Selkirk and District Angling Association a lease of the 'Haynings' salmon fishings from the right bank of the Ettrick for a five year term from the 1st January 2006. This lease will be upon the Crown Estate's standard terms and conditions and will be at a rent of £500 annually plus VAT. In the event that Selkirk and District Angling Association wish to enter into a subsequent lease of the 'Haynings' fishings after 1st January 2011 that lease would be based upon the commercial terms prevailing at that time.

Belford • Carlisle • Corbridge • Darlington • Dumfries • Edinburgh • Fochabers • Lichfield • Lincoln
London • Newmarket • Peterborough • Petworth • Preston • Winchester • Wrexham • York
Associated companies in British Virgin Islands • Denver • Kuala Lumpur • Sabah • Brunei

A list of partners is available from 17-18 Old Bond Street • London W1S 4PT • United Kingdom
Authorised and regulated by the Financial Services Authority. A member of primelocation.com

I shall be grateful if you would confirm that the points set out above accurately reflect the agreement between us. Meantime I am in touch with David Mitchell about the renunciation of the present lease held by the Angling Association and I have in hand preparation of the new lease of the 'Haynings' fishings.

Yours sincerely

Sir Robert M Clerk Bt. OBE FRICS
Consultant
e robert.clerk@smithsgore.co.uk • t Direct: 01968 677443

CC David Mitchell, Selkirk and District Angling Association
    Fiona Simpson, The Crown Estate

Victory!

Following the meeting in Selkirk, when the deal was done, this letter appeared to make the arrangements regarding Philiphaugh and Selkirk complete.

Appendix M

No. S. 2521.

Any reply to this letter should
be on foolscap paper, if convenient,
~~and should quote the above number~~
and the number of the File, and be
addressed to—
THE SECRETARY.

OFFICE OF WOODS, &c.,

1, WHITEHALL, S.W.,

19th June, 1912.

13

File S. 3627.

Gentlemen,

Salmon Fishings, River Ettrick.

In reply to your letter of the 17th instant I am
directed by Mr. Leveson Gower to state that the arrangement
with the Town Council of Selkirk is intended to be only
temporary and experimental.

This has been made clear in the correspondence.

The question of a lease has not yet been considere

I am,

Gentlemen,

Your obedient Servant,

Charles S. Hewlett

Joint Secretary.

HMW assure everyone that the arrangement is only temporary in 1912. It was never cancelled.

Appendix N

The start of the Haining Campaign

This is the letter on which the CEC partly based their claim to own the Haining's fishing rights. We had not researched the Haining rights as the length of river bank to which it related was only one-sided, roughly ½ a mile long and comprised only 10% of the total. Our principal aim was to secure Selkirk and Philiphaugh's rights and we had not yet fully appreciated the Haining stretch.

191

Appendix O

Letter from Haining lawyer re rebuttal of Haining adverse claim 2013

The Haining Charitable Trust

88-90   High   Street
Galashiels TD1 1SQ

T: 01896 668271
F: 01896 751 919

Email: susanedington@edingtonlaw.co.uk
Website: www.thehaining.co.uk

Mr Adam Borwick
Selkirk & District Angling Association
2 Dovecot Lane
Selkirk
TD7 4BF

*Our Ref:*SJE/ERH
Your Ref:
Date: 27 August 2013

Dear Adam

HAINING CHARITABLE TRUST

Thank you for forwarding your letter dated 19th August 2013. I previously went through this matter where it was clearly explicit that there was a Barony Title which included Salmon Fishings and I am afraid that I feel that the rebuttal of our claim was reasonable. I enclose a copy of the letter I received from Anderson Strathern and a copy of the information which they also forwarded to me. Please be aware of this and in the circumstances I feel that the cheque which you have made payable to us should in fact be paid to Crown Estates. I look forward to hearing from you in relation to this.

In the meantime, I have retained your cheque but not cashed same.

Yours sincerely

Registered Office: 88/90 High Street, Galashiels TD1 1SQ
A Charitable Company Limited by Guarantee. Registered in Scotland. Charity No.SC041505

This is the letter that we eventually got from the Haining lawyer – after all our work she sides with the Crown Estate! An incomprehensible act!

192

Appendix P
Rebuttal from the
CEC. p. 1.

Anderson Strathern LLP
1 Rutland Court
Edinburgh
EH3 8EY
Tel: +44 (0)131 270 7700
Fax: +44 (0)131 270 7788
DX ED3 Edinburgh 1
www.andersonstrathern.co.uk

Edingtons W.S.
88 High Street
Galashiels
TD1 1SQ

If calling, please ask for:	Jennifer Williams
Direct Dial:	0131 270 5287
Fax:	0131 625 8030
Email:	jennifer.williams@ andersonstrathern.co.uk

Our Ref: JCD\JZW2\CEC5000.91\JZW
Your Ref:

Date: **19 December 2012**

Dear Sirs

The Crown Estate
Haining Charitable Trust
Adverse Claim to Salmon Fishings in the River Ettrick, Haining Estate

We refer to previous correspondence on this matter and thank you for forwarding relevant title deeds to support an adverse claim to salmon fishing rights at the Haining River Ettrick. As you are aware the Haining salmon fishings have been let to the Selkirk and District Angling Association by The Crown Estate for many years. More recently the Association through their secretary Mr Mitchell has questioned The Crown Estate's ownership of the Beat suggesting that these were in fact owned by the late Mr Andrew Nimmo-Smith.

As you appreciate for an adverse claim to salmon fishings to be successful, the claimant must prove first, that they have a habile title to the salmon fishings and second, that such habile title has been followed by the requisite period of possession.

From your clients' title, the position is as follows:-

A Crown Charter of Confirmation in 1793 of the Barony of Haining included "the fishings" in the description of the Barony. This title constitutes a habile title to the salmon fishings and if it had been followed by the requisite 40 years possession with appropriate proof of such possession, an adverse claim would have been successful.

A Disposition by Anne Elizabeth Pringle Douglas or Pringle Pattison of Haining with consent in favour of herself (recorded GRS Selkirk 17 January 1870) of the Barony of Haining included only "fishings" but as it was a Barony title, again had there been the requisite 40 years possession with proof thereof, an adverse claim would have succeeded.

We carried out a search on Registers Direct and found that in 1940 there was a Disposition recorded on 27 June 1940 by the then owner of the Haining, Thomas Place, to the Provost,

92\1

193

2

Magistrates and Councillors of the Burgh of Selkirk of part of the Haining. This Disposition reserved "the fishings" within the River Ettrick to Thomas Place. In 1943 Thomas Place disponed the remainder of the Lands and Barony of Haining to Mark Fawdry including "trout fishings".

Mark Fawdry then transferred the Lands and Barony of Haining to Rodger (Builders) Limited on 5 August 1950 with no mention of fishings in the description shown on Registers Direct. However, given that only the trout fishings were transferred to Mark Fawdry by Thomas Place in 1943, he would only have had the ability to transfer the trout fishings and not the salmon fishings to Rodger (Builders) Limited.

Rodger (Builders) Limited transferred the Lands and Barony of Haining to Andrew Nimmo-Smith in 1961 with "trout fishings". The Lands and Barony of Haining was then transferred by the Executors of Andrew Nimmo-Smith to your clients by a Disposition recorded on 1 August 2012. We have not seen a copy of the 2012 Disposition.

As already mentioned, an adverse claim based on the 1793 Crown Charter or the 1870 Disposition would have been successful had the claimants been able to prove the requisite 40 years possession. We have gone to great lengths to investigate whether your clients' predecessors possessed the salmon fishings at the relevant time but we have been unsuccessful.

For example, we have examined the old Valuations Rolls from 1855 onwards to 1912 and have not found any evidence of rates having been paid for the salmon fishings in the River Ettrick *ex adverso* the Haining.

In addition we have examined our clients' historic records relating to salmon fishings in the River Ettrick. There is a letter of 20 October 1910 on file from Curle & Erskine WS, the solicitors of the then owners of the Haining. This letter, a copy of which is enclosed, is explicit in confirming that the Haining had no interest in the salmon fishings in the River Ettrick or its tributaries. It also shows that the owners of the Haining took legal advice before declining to submit an adverse claim to the salmon fishings in the River Ettrick *ex adverso* the Haining in 1910.

In addition, Mrs Pringle-Pattison is shown in the Particulars to Valuation Rolls on file as being the owner of the salmon fishings *ex adverso* Fairnalee in 1895 and also from 1870 to 1886. Copies of the relevant pages of the Particulars to Valuation Rolls are enclosed. From the titles we can see that Mrs Pringle-Pattison owned both Fairnalee and the Haining at that time, but there is no mention of the Haining in the Particulars from the Valuation Rolls as to Valuations. This corroborates the fact that Mrs Pringle-Pattison knew about title to salmon fishings and the requirement to pay rates thereon. She clearly knew she did not own the salmon fishings *ex adverso* the Haining, advisedly so given the letter from her solicitors of 20 October 1910.

The conclusion to be drawn is that the owners of the Haining, who are currently your clients, did not and do not own the salmon fishings in the River Ettrick *ex adverso* the Haining.

p. 3 of rebuttal letter from the CEC

The legal presumption that salmon fishings are within The Crown Estate's ownership has therefore not been rebutted and the salmon fishings in the River Ettrick *ex adverso* the Haining properly remain within the ownership of The Crown Estate.

Yours faithfully

Jim Drysdale
Partner
for and on behalf of Anderson Strathern LLP

cc. David Mitchell, Selkirk & District Angling Association

Appendix Q

Prescriptive possession

This is the legal device to confirm ownership of a property or right by its continued use "openly, peaceably and without judicial interruption" for varying lengths of time. (Currently 10 years, previously 20 years.) In salmon fishing the right has to be owned legally and then actually used in order for the Crown not to be able to claim the right as theirs.

One of the ways to own salmon fishing rights is:

> "By the prescriptive possession of salmon fishings by the holder of a barony title with or without fishings".

> And: "possession for twenty years is probably sufficient to establish prescription".

> *(Extracted from Green's Encyclopedia of the Law of Scotland, 2nd. Ed., 1911, Vol VI)*

Appendix R
Questions in the House of Commons

<u>Hansard</u>

ILLEGALLY CATCHING SALMON.

HC Deb 16 February 1893 vol 8 cc1570-1 <u>1570</u>

& <u>MR. THOMAS SHAW</u> (Hawick)

I beg to ask the Secretary for Scotland whether his attention has been called to the case of Bertram George Tyson, who were recently tried at Selkirk and sentenced each to pay a fine, including expenses, of £5 19s., or suffer 21 days' imprisonment, for being. in possession of salmon caught illegally; whether he is aware that there was absolutely no evidence in support of the charge of illegal fishing, and that this was admitted by the sheriff in giving judgment, and that the express ground of judgment was that it was no part of the prosecutor's duty to prove the guilt of the accused, but that it rested upon the accused to prove their innocence; and whether it is the intention of the Government to bring in a Bill to repeal the sections of "The <u>Tweed Fisheries Amendment Act, 1859</u>," which deprive accused persons of their ordinary rights at Common Law, or whether the Government will afford facilities to private Members for the introduction and passing of such a measure?

& <u>SIR G. TREVELYAN</u>

My attention has been called to the case of Bertram and George Tyson. (The offence was that of being in possession of salmon caught during close time and for, fishing otter than by rod and line.) By the terms of the Act the proof that the fish <u>1571</u> were not taken contrary to its provisions lay upon the accused, and, judging from the report of the proceedings which I have seen, I think the statement made in the second paragraph of the question is well founded. The many anomalies of the Tweed Acts, of which the present case furnishes one illustration, will receive the earliest attention which the Government can give them, and there is no reason whatever in the view of the Government why the Tweed Laws should be at all different from the general law on the subject. I may mention further that Mr. Gladstone's Government of 1886 had a Bill in preparation for the repeal of those provisions of the Tweed Acts to some of which the question refers.

Appendix S

Dr Lindsay D Neil MB ChB DA
Woodlands
Scotland

6/5/6

Mr Andrew Nimmo-Smith   *(delivered by hand to Mrs Cowan. I wasn't*
The Haining   *allowed to see Mr Nimmo-Smith)*

Dear Mr Nimmo-Smith,

Following my meeting with you and Mrs Cowan on Thursday last, I discussed with Sir David Steel and Sheriff Kevin Drummond what you said and what you were hoping to achieve with regard to the future of the house and estate in the event of your death.

We are all willing to act as 'founder' trustees to initiate and go through the formalities of setting up a trust to be named 'The Haining Trust' or some other name in order to secure the integrity and preservation of the estate in its entirety.

The objects of the trust would be educational, historical and recreational with an emphasis on wildlife and could be free-standing and separate from other existing organisations, Selkirk- based or otherwise, and thus provide protection from any depredations of developers. This last aim could be secured by a suitably worded Trust constitution. Charity status would be secured and grants would be sought from various sources for upkeep and development.

In order to take this idea further, we would need to know whether the house was proposed to be included and what the extent of the estate is. Furthermore, the name of your lawyer would be a prerequisite.

I shall call again next Thursday afternoon at 3 pm to see if this idea meets your objectives and whether therefore we should take the matter further.

Yours sincerely,

Selkirk Regeneration Group's suggestion about trust formation which was eventually adopted. No reply was received. Mrs Cowan was Mr Nimmo-Smith's carer and held Power of Attorney over his affairs.

Appendix T

Precis of correspondence 1910 to 1925 between HMW, various law firms, and Philiphaugh Estates.

Some 60 pages in all, a few missing. The bulk deals with negotiations that took place in 1912.

HMW were clearly anxious to regulate the unrestricted fishing in the Ettrick which had led to poaching, pollution and a general free-for-all. They wanted to establish a reasonable stretch of water which they hoped the Town Council would then lease from them and exert control over.

Philiphaugh Estate had previously been happy for anyone to fish their Water, but only with their tacit permission and reserved sanction. This was attested to in a witnessed declaration at the request of HMW. The barony rights were quoted as foundation. Their rights extended to both banks except for a portion on the South bank allegedly belonging to a Prof. Pringle-Pattison who, at the instigation of HMW, disclaimed his rights to fish it.

Voluminous correspondence ensued with HMW succeeding in confusing themselves and others over which cauld was which and where the marches were. It culminated in Philiphaugh not conceding their ownership, but agreeing as a concession, that HMW could lease both the Philiphaugh stretch and the town stretch to the Town Council. And thus HMW achieved their target of getting it regulated and controlled.

The ownership of Philiphaugh water was not resolved.

The bit on the south bank may belong to the Crown – unless we or Philiphaugh could claim prescriptive possession somehow. That could be a stickler. The rest as we have said, belongs to Philiphaugh.

Notable is a letter from HMW dated 19/6/1912 stating that the "arrangement with the Town Council of Selkirk is intended to be only **temporary and experimental**. …This has been made clear in the correspondence."

LDN 10 Feb 05

Appendix U

Synopsis of Correspondence between Lawyers, HMW, and Philiphaugh Estate, 1910 to 1925.

For convenience, the various letters have been re-arranged and assigned code numbers in the order they were received, **Pro 20 to 24 +/- capital letters.**

Abbreviations:

Lawyers, both acting for the estate:

DC & C Alexander, Selkirk. (DCA)

AJ & J Graham, Glasgow. (AJG)

Mr. Samuel Strang Steel. (SSS)

Selkirk Town Council. (STC)

HM Woods etc. (HMW)

Pro 23 A
18/11/1910,
Letter from HMW referring to earlier letter of 10/11/10 (missing) requesting a statutory declaration from Mr William Strang Steel that he had been in possession of the estate for 20+ years and that a barony title is held, that he exercised the rights of salmon fishing "to the exclusion of all other persons" and that he indicate on maps (missing) the banks on the river to which he claimed fishing rights.

23 B
22/11/10,
Letter from AJG to William Strang Steel enclosing **23A.**

23 C
24/12/10, Letter from DCA enclosing draft declaration referred to above.
(20A, emerges later)

Mr. William Strang Steel died **January 1911.**
No correspondence for that year.

20 A

19/2/12,

Draft declaration from SSS meeting the requirements of HMW in 23A – claiming rights to all the barony fishing rights and reserving the right to give permission to fish to anyone he wished. Defines the extent of his fishing rights (amended from his father's original 1910 draft).

22 A

27/2/12,

Letter from HMW acknowledging receipt of SSS's affidavit and suggesting SSS renounces the fishing rights between Murray's Cauld and Selkirk Bridge. Also questions the manner by which SSS gives permission to people to fish.

20 E&F

29/2/12,

Letter from DCA to AJG advising against HMW's suggestion of renouncement of fishing rights, refuting that permission to fish above the bridge was <u>not</u> by individual authorisation by his client (SSS). Questions ownership of fishing rights of Prof. Pringle-Pattison.

22 C

29/2/12,

Copies of 20 E & F.

20 D

2/3/12,

Letter from lawyers representing Prof. Pringle-Pattison renouncing his rights to fish the south bank between Murray's Cauld and where Philiphaugh's starts on the south bank.

22 E

4/3/12,

Letter from AJG to DCA confirming Prof. PP's renunciation and wanting more detail re the manner that fishing permission was given in the stretch above Selkirk bridge to pass on to HMW *(that was already covered in 20 E & F above).*

20 G & H, 22 F & G

5/3/12,

Letter from DCA to AJG restating claim to rights above bridge, but saying that SSS would consider renouncing his rights to fish from Murray's Cauld to the bridge <u>only</u> if the Crown would make him (SSS) a grant of the fishings at a nominal rent.

20 I & J, 22 H & I

8/3/12

Letter from AJG to HMW asserting Philiphaugh's fishing rights above the bridge and asserting that letting them to STC would be "detrimental to the estate". Concedes to HMW that SSS would be prepared to renounce all his fishing rights below the bridge.

20 K

8/3/12, same as above.

20 L & 22 J

12/3/12,

HMW replies rejecting SSS's offer to renounce rights below the bridge while retaining those above. Repeats request for SSS to renounce rights above bridge.

20 M & 22 K

13/3/12,

AJG to HMW registering strong objection to water between Murray's Cauld and bridge being let to STC. Repeats SSS's offer to renounce rights above and below bridge in return for grant of all fishings above bridge and nominal lease. ***This is important.***

20 N & 22 L

15/3/12,

HMW, for clarification, states that the object is to make it worthwhile for STC to lease a reasonable stretch of water and thereby control poaching etc. Concedes that HMW (Sir Stafford Howard) might consider a lease of the stretch above bridge to SSS along the lines contained in **20 M**. ***This is important.***

20 P & Q

18/3/12,

DCA to AJG restating that SSS's best interests are served by his pressing his ownership claim – *somewhat confused here* – but meaning that leasing the north bank to STC would not mean a lot to them (STC), but a great deal to SSS.

22 N, 20 R & S

22/3/12,

AJG to HMW pressing SSS's claim (as in 20 P & Q above) or alternatively again requesting a grant to the fishing above the bridge at nominal rent in order to protect his estate.

20,T,U,V & W.

21/3/12,

Handwritten letter from SSS to AJG acknowledging Sir Stafford Howard's offer to lease the stretch above the bridge of 15/3/12, "subject to my providing facilities by which the fishing may be exercised by the public under proper regulation". He says further; "I do not think it is worth my while to press any claim, nor do I think…I could substantiate a claim to the salmon fishings". Further, "I am inclined to give in".

20 Y

25/3/12,

Further handwritten note from SSS to AJG approving letter they wrote to HMW of 22/3/12 (22N, 20 R & S).

22 O

27/3/12,

HMW to AJG explaining some points and hoping that a temporary arrangement can be made.

22 P

28/3/12,

AJG reply to HMW, concurring with the temporary arrangement proposed "as an experiment", and inter alia, **"providing it is clearly understood that our client's claim to the fishings is not prejudiced"**.

23 F

2/4/12,

HMW to AJG, **acknowledging letter of 28/3/12** , (22P above) *but not specifically accepting contents*. Preparing the regulations which are not yet ready.

21

6/4/12,

DCA to AJG *a bit confused*, but wanted assurance that the proprietor would have the right to fish himself as would also the Estate workers. He also sought assurance that trout fishing was not interfered with "nor any other legal right".

23 G

17/4/12,

An incomprehensible letter from HMW to AJG considering the content of all the preceding correspondence.

Refers to the Crown having ownership of the "higher right of salmon fishing" to the Water in question.

23 H

30/4/12,

HMW to AJG undertaking to write further.

22 Q

15/6/12,

HMW to AJG referring to (23H) enclosing regulations (22R).

22 S

19/6/12,

HMW to AJG in reply to a (missing) letter dated 17/6/12 states that the arrangement with the **"Town Council of Selkirk is intended to be only temporary and experimental… This has been made clear in the correspondence"**.

22 T

18/6/12,

DCA to AJG, broadly approving the regulations.

Correspondence for 1912 ends.

24 A & B

1 November 1925

Letter from SSS to DCA questioning the future arrangements of the fishing lease having reviewed the files sent to him by AJG.

24 C

3 November 1925,

DCA to AJG returning files deciding to do nothing and observing that the "letters from HM Woods etc. seem almost farcical".

Conclusions:

1. At no point were the Philiphaugh rights given up. Offers to renounce portions were refused by HMW. The 1615 barony rights therefore still prevail.

2. Philiphaugh rights still extend below the bridge to the march with Linglie because HMW did not accept SSS's offer of their renunciation.

3. Despite receipt and acknowledgement of the affidavit, manifestly accepting its content and validity and subsequently trying to persuade SSS to renounce his fishing rights above the bridge, thereby acknowledging their validity, HMW <u>inexplicably</u> in **23 G**, after all the correspondence, reasserts the Crown's ownership of the fishing rights.

4. Philiphaugh Estate's proposal to HMW was that the Crown should lease to them the entire stretch above the bridge, including that previously belonging to Prof. PP to Philiphaugh Estate at a nominal rent, in return for Philiphaugh renouncing its own rights in the same stretch between Murray's Cauld and the bridge and, in addition, all rights below the bridge **(20 M, 22 N, 20 R & S)**.

   This was rejected **(20 L & 22 J)**.

5. The arrangement to allow HMW to lease to STC was ultimately acquiesced in by Philiphaugh **clearly reserving the rights to their fishings (22 P)**.

6. To all parties, the arrangements were agreed to be experimental and temporary only **(22 S)**.

7. For the convenience of their preferred arrangements, HMW then simply stole the Philiphaugh fishing rights by asserting they owned them.**(23 G)**.

Unresolved today is the ownership of the rights on the south bank between Murray's Cauld and where the property marches with Philiphaugh land. It is likely that the Crown recovered those rights by Prof. PP renouncing them and now owns them.

The Crown therefore probably legally owns the rights to approx. 1200 yards on the south bank below Murray's Cauld. On its own, this can have little value and would be near impossible to lease as a separate entity.

LDN 15/2/05.

BIBLOGRAPHY

References

1. <u>Liber Saint Marie de Calchou:</u> (The book of Kelso) written c. 1330. Contains transcriptions of the erecting charters for Selkirk and Kelso abbeys. There are references to 'fishings' in relation to Monastic rights to do so but it also clearly refers to the same rights obtaining for the people living in the royal demesne of Selkirk. Three identical references, AD 1119, 1147 – 1152 and 1159. Rights granted by Earl David, King David I and King Malcolm IV. Relevant charters/pages & P/C of translation are preserved in Floors Castle Archives & Advocates Library, Edinburgh History of Selkirkshire, by T Craig Brown. Edinburgh 1886. pp.383 et seq.

2. <u>Valuation Rolls for Selkirk 1714.</u> Quoted from 'Selkirk 1714, by Walter Elliot, 1981. p. 33. Specifies that the 'Comonties' ie. 'property held in common' * by the Burgh is assessed at £1000 (Scots). No rent or charge to Burghers for fishing is identified in the text indicating that none was appropriate, the rights to fishings being held in 'Common' by all the citizens of the Burgh.

3. <u>Scots Burgh Finances Prior to 1707.</u> Unpublished PhD thesis, GS Pryde, St Andews 1926. Defines the:"chief concrete rights of burgesses is the possession of the burgh itself with a certain amount of 'real property' around the burgh such as fields, pastures, meadows. mills, ponds, **fishings**, peat-bogs and quarries". A similar description of Burgh rights is found in 'Mercat Cross and Tolbooth' by Craig Mair, Edinburgh, 1988. p.85. (photocopy)

4. <u>History of Selkirkshire – Court Book.</u> Not yet published. Entry of 21st Sept 1541. Line of marches – this shows that the Common Lands included the fields to the East of the present Bridgeheugh House. Walter Mason Papers, Selkirk Museum.

5. <u>Photocopies of minutes of Selkirk Burgh Council, 31/1/1910 to 7/9/1914.</u> All minutes dealing with the claim by 'HM Woods etc.' that the Crown owned the fishing rights on the Ettrick. Summary of entries. Photocopies. Originals in Municipal Buildings, Galashiels.

6. <u>The Tourist's Guide and Angler's Companion (photocopy)</u>
   By James Crichton and Thomas Wight. Selkirk 1893.
   While dealing mainly with trout fishing, the catching of salmon on the Ettrick is recounted. The author would not be publishing a confession to illegal fishing! Pp. 123, 130,138 & 140 refer.

7. <u>Boundaries of Selkirk North Common</u>. Photocopy of entry dated 21 Sept 1541 of Selkirk Council minutes. Craig Brown, Vol.II, pp. 42 & 43.

8. <u>Extract from Green's Encyclopedia of the Law of Scotland</u>, 2nd. Ed., 1911, Vol VI. (Photocopy) This underlines that the ownership of fishing rights accompanies a Barony charter, especially if specifically mentioned. States also that any references to 'fishings' can mean salmon fishings. Page 11.

9. <u>Stair Memorial Encyclopaedia, 1990, Vol 11.</u> (Photocopy)
Confirms (8) above, and specifically mentions the use of 'Piscariis' to mean Salmon fishing. Page 2, Para.4, (2) & (4).

10. <u>Charter of King James I/VI 1615.</u> Granting Barony of Phillopehaugh to Sir John Murray. Specifically grants land 'cum piscariis'. (Photocopy) shows that the fishing rights were disposed of by the Crown in 1615. The Barony still exists, but has not been matriculated for two generations. The current estate owner, Sir Michael Strang Steel, now owns the fishing rights to 4 miles of the Ettrick/Yarrow part of which the Crown has claimed since 1910. The Charter was not recorded in 'The Register of the Great Seal' 1912 edition, and only discovered in Edinburgh in 2000. (original possessed)

11. <u>Advertisement of Sale of Philiphaugh Estate 1885.</u> Details salmon fishing is included in sale. (Photocopy).

12. <u>Particulars of sale of Philiphaugh Estate, 1888.</u> Confirms (11) above.(Photocopy). Attached map shows boundaries of the estate. (OS 1885)

13. <u>James V Charter, 1535/36.</u> Re-affirmation of Burgh Status to Selkirk. 'with the commons and possessions......in the same manner as any other burgh within the kingdom'. Craig Brown, Vol II, p.38.

14. <u>Synopsis of Lease between HM Woods etc & Selkirk Burgh Council.</u> 6 Oct 1914. (Photocopy)

15. <u>Letter to Ian Brown from Prof. W M Gordon</u> giving an opinion on the validity of a claim by Selkirk to have owned the fishing rights in 'common'. dtd.11 Feb 1993. Indecisive re value of the charters.

16. <u>Selkirk Council Minutes 1713.</u> showing the council had responsibility to maintain the integrity of the structures in the Ettrick within the Burgh. "the hail inhabitants, having horse or no having" ordered to go with "sufficient utensils for carrying stones, heather, whins etc., to stay the new current", to save the threatened cauld. Craig Brown, Vol II, p.89.

17. <u>Barony of Gallaschielles 12 may 1797</u>: reference to 'Boldside with fishings', without reference to 'salmon'. Subsequent reference makes clear that 'fishing' refers to salmon fishing. Craig Brown, Vol II, p391.

18. <u>Statistical Account, Dr Douglas of Galashiels</u> 1798, Salmon described as 'food of the people' and sold at 6d/lb or 1½d/lb if 'less fresh'. There is no mention of charges being made 'to fish'.

    Craig Brown, Vol II, p.411.

19. <u>Public Notice 1806</u>. Issued by the Procurator fiscal, George Rodger of Selkirk. Comprehensively defines contraventions and penalties relating to fishing outside the permitted times and other offences. No mention is made of those not entitled to fish, fishing dues or regulations pertaining thereto. Photograph - Walter Mason Papers, Selkirk Museum.

20. <u>Notice 1817</u> issued by the same Procurator fiscal. It mentions those 'without having any proper leave or authority' to fish. This confirms that the legal authorities of Selkirk had jurisdiction over who had the right to fish in the Selkirkshire waters. No fishing dues are mentioned. Photograph – Walter Mason Papers, Selkirk Museum.

21. <u>Map of Fishings</u> currently let by the Crown to Selkirk Angling Association.

22. <u>Calendar of Documents Relating to Scotland</u>, ed. of Bain, (Edinburgh 1881 to 1888). Vol. V. ed. J Galbraith. ii 1839, v 492 xii.

23. <u>The Acts of the Parliament of Scotland</u>, ed., T. Thomson, C. Innes, (Edinburgh, 1814 – 1875). ii, 568. SBC Library Archives.

24. <u>Flower of the Forest</u>, ed. John M. Gilbert, Selkirk Common Good Fund, 1985. p. 81. (photocopy)

25. <u>The Acts of the Parliament of Scotland</u> viii, 419 to 428.
    This act 'till all time comeing', specifies rights belonging to the Burgh 'from comonties to property' with reference to the South Common. SBC Library Archives.

26. <u>Local government (Scotland) Act, 1974.</u> SBC Library Archives.

27. <u>The Douglas Book.</u> 1886, (Sir William Fraser) III, 36. National Library of Scotland, George IV Bridge.

28. <u>Registrum Magnum Sigilli Regum Scottorum</u>. 1593 – 1608, No. 1283. Scottish Borders Council Library HQ. Selkirk.

29. <u>Book of Melrose</u>. No. 548 & 3.

30. Personal Communication from the secretary of Selkirk Angling Association.

31. Selkirk Burgh Accounts: various years from 1644 to 1766.
    SC/S/12/23 and D/4//1/2. SBC Library Archives.

32. 'Accompte of the Common Goods' 1696.
    SC/3/12/25/2. SBC Library Archives.

33. Burgh records including Valuation 1712. 'The Town's Commons' valued
    At £ 1160 'Scotts'. D/4/6/1 & 2. SBC Library Archives.

34. Burgh Treasurer's Receipts, 1594 to 1773
    SC/S/12/26/ 1 to 315. SBC Library Archives.

35. Burgess, Merchant and Priest, Birlinn, ISBN 1 84158 147x, 2002. p.6.

36. Selkirk Burgh Valuation Rolls; 1712, 1714, 1715 & 1721. Selkirk Poll Tax Roll 1694. D/4/11/1 to 5.
    SBC Library Archives.

37. Selkirk Burgh Valuation Rolls; 1695 & c.1712. SC/S/12/25/ 1 & 2,
    SBC Library Archives

38. Scots Law Times, LA vs McCulloch, 1875 2R 27.

39. History of Selkirkshire by Thomas Craig Brown.
    Douglas, Edinburgh 1886.Vols 1 & 2

40 Selkirk Burgh Court Book;
    Published by the Stair Society 1960 Vol II Pages 187 & 188.